# English for
## the Oil industry

**1**

**Vocational English
Course Book**

Evan Frendo with David Bonamy

Series editor David Bonamy

# Contents

- Introduce yourself and others
- Talk about getting oil to the customer and oil fields around the world
- Talk about jobs in the oil industry
- Say the letters of the alphabet
- Talk about personal protective equipment (PPE)

## Introductions

**Listening**

**1** 🔊 **02** Listen and read. Match the texts 1–5 with the pictures A–E.

I am → I'm
You are → You're
He/She/It is → He's/
   She's/It's
We are → We're
You are → You're
They are → They're

1 Hi. My name is Armando Panganiban. I'm from the Philippines. I'm a driver. *E*
2 Hello. My name's Ricardo Cabrera. I'm from Venezuela. I'm a roustabout.
3 I'm Ali bin Khalid, from Saudi Arabia. I'm an engineer. Nice to meet you.
4 Hi, I'm Jennifer Burgess. I'm from Scotland. I'm a radio operator.
5 Hello. I'm Matthew Aondoakaa from Nigeria. I'm a seismic operator.

**A**
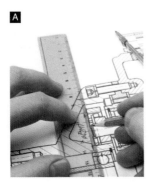

**B**

**C**

**D**

**E**

**Speaking**

**2** Practise the conversation in pairs.

A: What's your name?    B: Armando Panganiban.
A: Where are you from?    B: I'm from the Philippines.
A: What do you do?    B: I'm a driver.

**3** Practise in pairs. Ask and answer questions about Ricardo Cabrera, Ali bin Khalid, Jennifer Burgess and Matthew Aondoakaa. Then find a different partner and repeat.

# Getting oil to the customer

**1**  🔊 **03**  Listen. Write the names under the photos.

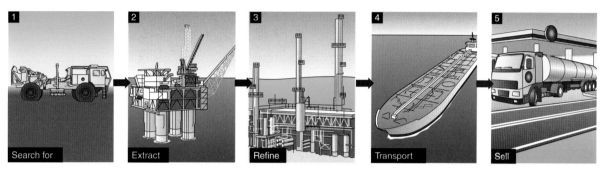

| 1 | 2 | 3 | 4 | 5 |
| Search for | Extract | Refine | Transport | Sell |

_Matthew Aondoakaa_ ......................... ......................... ......................... .........................

**Vocabulary** **2** Complete the table.

| Name | Job | Work location |
| --- | --- | --- |
| Armando Panganiban | | |
| Ricardo Cabrera | _roustabout_ | |
| Ali bin Khalid | | _refinery_ |
| Jennifer Burgess | _radio operator_ | |
| Matthew Aondoakaa | | |

**3** Are these sentences true (T) or false (F)?

1 Armando is a driver. He drives a road tanker. T/F
2 Matthew works on an oil rig. T/F
3 Ricardo is a roustabout. T/F
4 Ali is an engineer at a refinery. T/F
5 Jennifer is a radio operator on an oil rig. T/F

**Language**

### Present simple

| We use the **present simple** to talk about something that is always or usually true. | I/You/We/They **work** on an oil rig / at the refinery / in Nigeria. |
| --- | --- |
| | He/She **works** on an oil rig / at the refinery / in Nigeria. |

### Present simple of *be*

| The **present simple** of *be* is irregular. | I **am** a driver. |
| --- | --- |
| | You/We / They **are** a driver / drivers. |
| | He / She **is** a driver. |

**4** Talk about your classmates.

*Richard Smith is from Alaska. He's a driver. He works in …*

# Spelling

**1** ▶ 🎧 **04** Listen and repeat.

> **The alphabet**
> A, H, J, K
> B, C, D, E, G, P, T, V, Z (American English)
> F, L, M, N, S, X, Z (British English)
> I, Y
> O
> Q, U, W
> R

**2** ▶ 🎧 **05** Listen and fill in the missing letters.

1 _e_ _n_ g _i_ n _e_ _e_ r
2 _ _ e _ _ t _ _
3 _ _ i _ _ r
4 _ _ u _ t _ b _ _ t
5 _ e _ _ _ _ e _ y
6 _ _ l _ _ g
7 _ _ n _ _ r

**3** ▶ 🎧 **06** Listen and read.

1 A: Hello. My name's Cabrera. That's C-A-B-R-E-R-A.
  B: Thank you.
2 A: Panganiban.
  B: How do you spell that?
  A: It's Panganiban. P-A-N-G-A-N-I-B-A-N.
  B: Thank you.
3 A: Matthew Aondoakaa.
  B: Pardon?
  A: Aondoakaa. That's A-O-N-D-O-A-K-double A.
  B: Thank you.

**4** ▶ 🎧 **07** Underline the items you hear.

PPE    API    KV    RPM    VDU    CO    USA    UAE    TSR

**5** Practise in pairs. Ask and answer questions like those below. Then change partners and repeat.

A: *What's your name?*
B: *Smith.*
A: *How do you spell that?*
B: *S-M-I-T-H.*
A: *Thank you.*

# Jobs

**Reading**  **1**  Read about different crews. Match the texts to the pictures of the jobs.

1  I work on a supertanker. We have a crew of 25. We live on the ship. The captain's in charge. We transport the oil. *D*

2  Here is my crew. We live and work on an oil rig. The driller is in charge. He's the boss. We extract the oil. I'm a roustabout.

3  Our crew is small. We have a surveyor and three seismic operators. We search for oil. We work in the countryside.

4  The refinery is big. I work in the control room. I supervise the control room operators so I'm the supervisor. We control the refinery. We refine the oil.

**Listening**  **2**  🎧 **08**  Listen and write down the words you hear.

1  We _transport_ the oil.
2  We _____ the oil.
3  We _____ for oil.
4  We _____ the oil.
5  I work on a _____ .
6  We work on an _____ .
7  We work in the _____ .
8  We work in the _____ .
9  I'm the _____ .
10  I'm the _____ .
11  I'm a _____ .
12  I'm a _____ operator.
13  I'm a _____ .
14  I'm a _____ operator.

**Speaking**  **3**  Practise in pairs. Talk about the pictures. Don't read the texts.

*This man works in the refinery control room. He supervises … .*

# Introducing yourself and others

**1** 🔊 09 Listen to and read the conversations.

---

**Conversation 1**

John: Hi. Welcome to the crew. My name's John. I'm the driller, so I'm in charge of this crew.

Ahmed: Thanks. I'm Ahmed.

John: This is Harry. And that's Martin. They're roughnecks.

Ahmed: Excuse me. Roughnecks?

John: Roughnecks. They do all the general jobs.

Ahmed: Oh, OK.

---

**Conversation 2**

Sayed: Hello. I'm Sayed. I'm the new control room operator.

Brian: Oh, good to see you, Sayed. I'm Brian. I'm the supervisor. This is Frank. He's an operator, too.

Sayed: Hi, Frank.

Frank: Hello, Sayed.

---

**Conversation 3**

Manuel: Hi. I'm looking for Fred. I'm Manuel.

Fred: Hi. I'm Fred. Are you the new radio operator?

Manuel: Yes, that's right.

Fred: Oh, good. Come with me. I'll show you the radio room.

---

**Conversation 4**

Antonio: Hello. My name's Antonio.

Chris: Pardon?

Antonio: Antonio.

Chris: Hi, Antonio. I'm Chris. Are you the new surveyor?

Antonio: Yes, that's right. Antonio Rivaldi.

Chris: Good to meet you. I'm a surveyor, too.

---

→
*Roughneck? → What is a roughneck?*

→
*Pardon? → Please repeat.*

**2** Read the conversations again. What is the difference between the words in red and the words in blue in Conversation 1? Find similar phrases in Conversations 2, 3 and 4.

## Language

**Asking questions**

| We use **questions** to get information. The word order in questions is different from positive and negative sentences and we can use special questions words. | *Is he the supervisor?* |
| --- | --- |
| | *Are you John?* |
| | *What's your name?* |
| | *What do you do?* |
| | *Where do you work?* |
| | *How do you spell that?* |

**3** Read the conversations above again. Underline the questions.

**4** Practise in pairs. Ask and answer questions about Harry, Martin, Sayed, Brian, Frank, Manuel, Fred, Antonio and Chris.

*What **does** he do?*
*→ What's his job?*

A: *Where does John work?*
B: *He works on an oil rig.*
A: *What does he do?*
B: *He's a driller.*

---

8 | **1** The oil industry

# Health and safety: Personal protective equipment (PPE)

**Vocabulary**   **1**   Look at these pictures. Say the words.

Gloves  *1*         Safety glasses  ☐         Helmet  ☐

Boots  ☐         Ear protectors  ☐         Trousers  ☐         Jacket  ☐

**Listening**   **2**    🔊 **10**   Listen and write the correct number next to the pictures above.

       **3**    🔊 **11**   Listen and write down the PPE items you hear.

1   *ear protectors* _____
2   _____
3   _____
4   _____
5   _____

**Speaking**   **4**   Look at the picture and label the PPE items. Then practise in pairs. Ask and answer questions about PPE items.

    A: *What does a helmet protect?*
    B: *It protects the head.*
    A: *What do gloves protect?*
    B: *They protect the hands.*

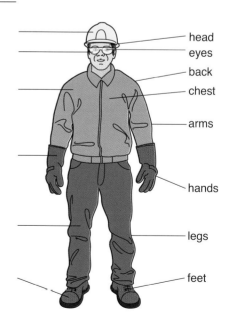

head
eyes
back
chest
arms
hands
legs
feet

# Oil fields

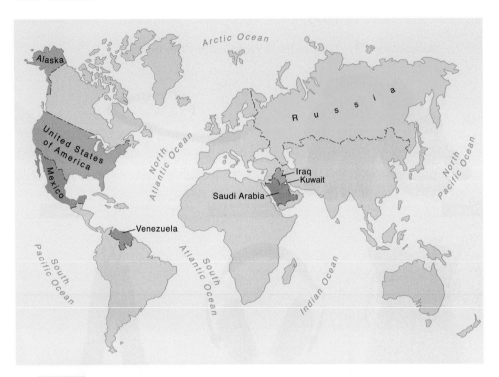

**1**  ▶ 🎵 12  Listen and mark the stress. Then repeat.

1  Ven<u>e</u>zuela
2  Mexico
3  USA
4  Saudi Arabia
5  Kuwait
6  Alaska
7  Iraq
8  Russia

**2**  ▶ 🎵 13  Listen. Match the oil fields to the countries or state.

**Oil fields**                                         **Countries or state**

1  Samotlor                                            a)  Venezuela

2  Prudhoe Bay                                         b)  Mexico

3  East Texas                                          c)  USA

4  Cantarell                                           d)  Saudi Arabia

5  Greater Burgan                                      e)  Kuwait

6  Rumaila                                             f)  Alaska

7  Ghawar                                              g)  Iraq

8  Bolivar Coastal                                     h)  Russia

**Speaking**  **3**  Practise in pairs. Test yourselves. Then find a new partner and repeat.

A:  *Where is Ghawar?*
B:  *I think Ghawar is in Saudi Arabia.*
A:  *Where is East Texas?*
B:  *I'm sure East Texas is in the USA.*

# Review

**Writing**

**1** Use *what* or *where* to complete the questions.

1 *Where* _____ do you work?
2 _____ do you do?
3 _____'s my helmet?
4 _____'s a roughneck?
5 _____'s your name?
6 _____ are you from?
7 _____ does he do?

**2** Label the pictures with the words in the box.

| extract | search for | refine | ~~sell~~ | transport |
|---------|------------|--------|----------|-----------|

 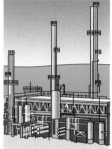   

1 *sell* .............

2 .....................

3 .....................

4 .....................

5 .....................

**3** Find the names of six more countries and one state.

| g | j | g | e | y | a | e | d | k | c | v |
|---|---|---|---|---|---|---|---|---|---|---|
| m | e | x | i | c | o | r | f | u | v | e |
| t | h | i | d | x | s | g | c | w | p | n |
| h | u | o | f | r | a | b | r | a | x | e |
| k | s | p | s | z | l | n | u | i | l | z |
| v | a | l | i | r | a | q | s | t | k | u |
| c | g | j | g | i | s | m | s | u | y | e |
| a | e | a | h | o | k | k | i | h | j | l |
| s | a | u | d | i | a | r | a | b | i | a |

**4** Complete the texts. Then go to page 7 to check your answers.

1 I work on a super (1) *tanker* _____ . We have a crew of 25. We live on the (2) _____ . The Captain's (3) _____ charge. We transport the oil.

2 The refinery is big. I work in the control (4) _____ . I supervise the control room operators. I'm a (5) _____ . We control the refinery. We refine the (6) _____ .

**5** Write down five of each of these.

1 PPE items
2 parts of the body
3 jobs in the oil industry
4 things about yourself

# Looking for oil

- Talk about looking for oil
- Use numbers (1 to 100)
- Say where things are
- Understand and give simple instructions
- Give personal information

## On land

**Reading** **1** Read the text and underline words from the diagram.

Seismic operators search for oil. On land we use a <u>thumper truck</u>. The thumper truck carries heavy plates. Heavy plates are the energy source. The heavy plates hit the ground and make shock waves. Sometimes we use explosives. The explosion is the energy source. The explosion sends shock waves through the rock. The layers of rock reflect the waves to the receiver. We call these reflected waves. We use computers in the recording truck to record the data and to analyse the data.

Explosives

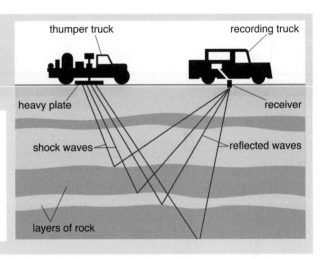

thumper truck     recording truck

heavy plate     receiver

shock waves     reflected waves

layers of rock

**Vocabulary** **2** Match the words 1–6 with the words a–f to make partnerships.

| | | | |
|---|---|---|---|
| 1 | thumper | a) | operator |
| 2 | energy | b) | source |
| 3 | shock | c) | plate |
| 4 | recording | d) | truck |
| 5 | seismic | e) | wave |
| 6 | heavy | f) | truck |

**Listening** **3** 🔊 **14** Listen. Write down the words you hear. Read the words aloud.

**Speaking** **4** Practise in pairs. Use the diagram. Ask and answer questions.

A: *What's this?*
B: *It's a heavy plate.*
A: *What does it do?*
B: *It hits the ground and makes shock waves.*

B: *What are these?*
A: *They're shock waves.*
B: *What do they do?*
A: *They go through the rock.*

# At sea

**Reading**   1   Complete the text with words from the diagram.

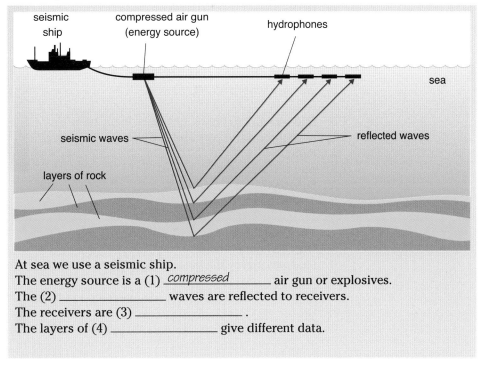

seismic ship    compressed air gun (energy source)    hydrophones

sea

seismic waves    reflected waves

layers of rock

At sea we use a seismic ship.
The energy source is a (1) _compressed_ air gun or explosives.
The (2) _____ waves are reflected to receivers.
The receivers are (3) _____ .
The layers of (4) _____ give different data.

**Listening**   2   ▶ 🔊 15   Listen and mark the stress. Then listen again and repeat the words.

1   <u>hy</u>drophones           4   energy
2   reflected              5   explosives
3   receiver               6   different

**Writing**   3   Write the words in the correct order.

1   At sea seismic we a use ship .
2   The energy source is explosives compressed gun air a or .
3   The waves are to reflected receivers .
4   The receivers hydrophones are .
5   The layers of different rock give data .

4   Complete the text.

_____ operators work on land and at sea. On land the energy
source is a _____ plate or an explosion. At sea the energy
source is a _____ air gun. The waves from the energy source
hit the _____ of rock and are reflected to receivers. Computers
_____ and analyse the data.

**Speaking**   5   Practise in pairs. Explain how seismic operators search for oil on land and at sea. Draw diagrams to help.

*On land seismic operators use thumper trucks. At sea they use seismic ships. ...*

# Seismic operators

**1**  **16** Listen to and read the conversation.

A: Hi, Matthew.

B: Hi.

A: What do you do?

B: I'm a seismic operator.

A: What do seismic operators do?

B: Well, we search for oil.

A: OK.

B: And we work in crews, or teams. In my crew we have three surveyors and five seismic operators.

A: Right.

B: And two shooters.

A: Shooters?

B: That's right. Shooters.

A: What do they do?

B: They handle the explosives.

A: Oh, OK. I understand.

B: First, we survey the land. We look for the best places to go.

A: I see.

B: Then we clear the land. We remove trees and bushes, for example.

A: OK.

B: Then we do our tests. We operate thumper trucks. The heavy plates send shock waves into the rock. We use receivers to record the data and we use computers to analyse the data.

A: What about the shooters?

B: The shooters? Well, sometimes we don't use thumper trucks. Sometimes we use explosives. The shooters drill holes into the ground and prepare the site. Then they detonate the explosives. The explosives send shock waves through the rock. We use receivers to record the data from the shock waves. Then we use computers to analyse the data.

A: Do you like your job?

B: Yeah, I do.

**2** Find verbs that go with these nouns.

1 _handle_ explosives    5 _____ shock waves

2 _____ land           6 _____ data

3 _____ tests          7 _____ holes

4 _____ thumper trucks

**Language**

### Plurals

| There are three different ways to make regular **plurals**: add -s, add -es or remove the y and add -ies. Some plurals are irregular. | truck → truck**s** |
| | bush → bush**es** |
| | country → countr**ies** |
| | foot → feet |

### Pronunciation

/s/ /z/ or /ɪz/

/s/  plates, shooters

/z/  waves, eyes

/ɪz/  bushes

**3** Read the conversation again. Underline the questions Then practise in pairs. Ask and answer these questions.

1 What do seismic operators do?

2 What do surveyors do?

3 What do shooters do?

# Numbers

**Language**

**Numbers 1 to 100**

| | | | | | |
|---|---|---|---|---|---|
| 1 | one | 11 | eleven | 21 | twenty-one |
| 2 | two | 12 | twelve | 22 | twenty-two |
| 3 | three | 13 | thirteen | 30 | thirty |
| 4 | four | 14 | fourteen | 40 | forty |
| 5 | five | 15 | fifteen | 50 | fifty |
| 6 | six | 16 | sixteen | 60 | sixty |
| 7 | seven | 17 | seventeen | 70 | seventy |
| 8 | eight | 18 | eighteen | 80 | eighty |
| 9 | nine | 19 | nineteen | 90 | ninety |
| 10 | ten | 20 | twenty | 100 | one hundred |

**Pronunciation**

Note the difference between:
thir<u>teen</u> (13) and <u>thir</u>ty (30)
four<u>teen</u> (14) and <u>for</u>ty (40)
six<u>teen</u> (16) and <u>six</u>ty (60)

**Listening**

**1** 17 Listen and circle the numbers you hear.

a) 4 14 (40)
b) 3 13 30
c) 12 14 16 60
d) 2 12 22 32
e) 9 19 49 99

**2** 18 Listen and write the numbers you hear.

a) *five*
b) ________
c) ________ , ________
d) ________ , ________ , ________
e) ________ , ________ , ________
f) ________ , ________
g) ________ , ________ , ________
h) ________ , ________

**Writing**

**3** What's next? Write the answer and compare in pairs.

a) 1, 2, 3, *4*
b) 3, 5, 7, ______
c) 2, 4, 6, ______
d) 9, 10, 11, ______
e) 20, 30, 40, ______
f) 19, 18, 17, ______

**4** Write the numbers.

a) forty-one *41*
b) twenty-three ______
c) thirty-nine ______
d) thirteen ______
e) twelve ______
f) seventy-four ______

**Speaking**

**5** Say the following three times, as fast as possible. Then make up similar 'tongue twisters'.

a) Three thumper trucks
b) Sixty-six seismic operators
c) Forty-four hydrophones

**6** Practise in pairs. Take turns to give instructions.

*A:* *Count from one to ten.*
*B:* *OK. One, two, three, four, five, six, seven, eight, nine, ten. Now your turn. Count backwards from eighty-seven to seventy-eight.*
*A:* *OK. Eighty-seven, eighty-six, eighty-five, …*

# Where is it?

**Vocabulary** **1** Look at the picture. Read the sentences about the picture.

1 The safety manual is on the table.
2 The boots are under the table.
3 The safety glasses are next to the manual.
4 The helmet is on the floor, between the table and the door.
5 My jacket is behind the door, on the hook.
6 The table is in front of the window.
7 The coffee is in the cup.

**Writing** **2** Complete the sentences.

1 Where's the helmet?
  It's _on_____ the floor, _____ the table and the door.
2 Where's the jacket?
  It's _____ the door, _____ the hook.
3 Where's the coffee?
  It's _____ the cup.
4 Where are the glasses?
  They're _____ the manual.
5 Where are the boots?
  They're _____ the table.
6 Where's the manual?
  It's _____ the table.

**Speaking** **3** Practise in pairs. Use things in the room.

*A: Where are the keys?*
*B: They're on the table.*

Pen

Keys

Mobile phone

Cupboard

Bottle of water

Window

# Health and safety: Instructions

**Vocabulary** **1** Practise in pairs. Take turns to give and follow instructions.

1 Stand up. Don't stand up. Sit down.
2 Point to the door. Don't point to the door. Point to the window.
3 Wave. Don't wave. Touch your head.
4 Stand near the door. Don't stand near the door. Stand near the window.
5 Turn on the lights. Turn off the lights.
6 Don't put your book under the table. Put your book on the table.

> **Don't** touch. → Do not touch.
> **Don't** do that. → Do not do that.

**Listening** **2** 🔊 **19** Listen to and read the conversation.

| | |
|---|---|
| Shooter: | OK, your first job. Explosives are dangerous, so be careful. |
| Assistant: | OK. |
| Shooter: | First of all, turn off that phone. No phones with explosives. |
| Assistant: | Sorry. |
| Shooter: | No problem. Now. Bring the box over here. |
| Assistant: | OK. |
| Shooter: | And put the spare cables on the truck. Yellow on the right, red on the left. |
| Assistant: | OK. |
| Shooter: | And keep an eye on the road. Any cars, call me. OK? |
| Assistant: | OK. |
| Shooter: | And don't touch that flask. It's my coffee. Not yours! |
| Assistant: | OK! |

**3** Complete the instructions with the words in the box.

> bring    be    ~~turn~~    keep    put    touch

1 _turn_ _____ off the phone.
2 _____ the box here.
3 _____ careful.
4 _____ the cables on the truck.
5 _____ an eye on the road.
6 Don't _____ the flask.

**Language**

**Instructions**

| We use the infinitive without *to* to give **instructions**. | ***Turn on*** *the lights.* |
| --- | --- |
| | ***Turn off*** *that phone.* |
| | ***Stand*** *up.* |
| | ***Sit*** *down.* |
| We add ***please*** to make the instructions more polite. | *Please **don't touch**.* |
| | *Please **turn on** the lights.* |
| | ***Sit*** *down, please.* |

**4** Play 'Simon says'. Your teacher will explain the game.

# Giving personal information

Listening **1** ▶ 🔊 20 Listen and repeat the telephone numbers.

    a) 0780 786 3487      b) 675 489 955      c) 546 389 2001

**2** ▶ 🔊 21 Listen and correct these numbers.

    a) 030 3562 8988 7          d) 030 456 347 328
    b) 0071 253 628 998        e) 0786 747 636 468
    c) 0049 756 463 839

**3** ▶ 🔊 22 Listen and complete the conversations.

**Conversation 1**

A: What's your
   (1) _name_ ?
B: Jason Henley.
A: Is Jason your given name?
B: Yes, Henley is my family name.
A: OK. Where do you
   (2) _____ ?
B: My address is 27 Port Drive, Aberdeen.
A: Did you say 27?
B: Yes, that's right.
A: And how old are you,
   (3) _____ ?
B: I'm 28.
A: 28? OK. Good. What's your job?
B: I'm a (4) _____ on an oil rig.
A: Thank you.

**Conversation 2**

A: What's your name, please?
B: John Karuett.
A: Can you (5) _____ that, please?
B: Yes, sure. It's John, J-O-H-N, Karuett, K-A-R-U-E-double T.
A: Thank you. And your (6) _____ ?
B: 45 Julienne Street.
A: OK. Postcode?
B: 24351.
A: Age?
B: (7) _____ .
A: Height?
B: Six foot one.
A: Weight?
B: 93 kilos.
A: OK. And what do you do?
B: I'm a shooter?
A: Pardon?
B: A shooter. I work with (8) _____ .
A: OK. Thank you.

**4** Complete the table. The third column is for you.

| Given name | Jason | John | You |
|---|---|---|---|
| Family name | | | |
| Address | | | |
| Telephone number | | | |
| Age | | | |
| Job | | | |
| Height | | | |
| Weight | | | |

Speaking **5** Practise in pairs. Ask and answer questions.

A: *What's your telephone number?*     B: *It's 2345 67876. And yours?*
A: *It's 34556786. How old are you?*     B: *I'm 23. And you?*
A: *I'm 31. How tall are you?*     B: *I'm five foot eleven inches. And you? What's your height?*
A: *I'm five foot seven inches. How heavy are you?*     B: *I'm 88 kilos. And you? What's your weight?*
A: *I'm 99 kilos.*

# Review

**1**   Write the plurals.

1   flask        _____        5   inch        _____
2   bush         _____        6   shooter     _____
3   explosive    _____        7   country     _____
4   operator     _____

**2**   Write these numbers in words.

1   15   _____        4   56   _____
2   16   _____        5   73   _____
3   34   _____        6   98   _____

**3**   Label these diagrams.

A

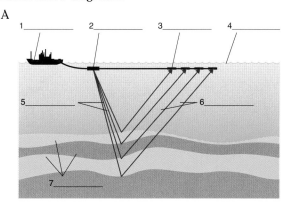

B

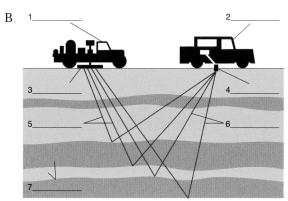

**4**   What do shooters do? Write three sentences.

**5**   Write six sentences about the room.

*The cell phone is on the table. The door is open.*

**6**   Write the opposite.

1   Stand up.              *Don't stand up. / Sit down.* _____
2   Turn on the phone.     _____
3   Touch the table.       _____
4   Point to the door.     _____
5   Wave.                  _____
6   Put the book on the table.   _____

# Oil fields

- Talk about oil field equipment
- Give and understand instructions for operating equipment
- Describe control panels
- Tell the time
- Understand warning signs
- Make conversation

## Oil field equipment

**Vocabulary** 1 ▶ 🔊 23 Listen and write down the labels for the pictures.

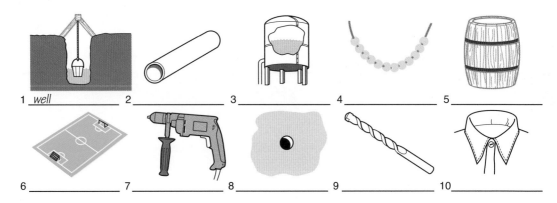

1 _well_ 2 _____ 3 _____ 4 _____ 5 _____

6 _____ 7 _____ 8 _____ 9 _____ 10 _____

2 Label these diagrams with the words in the box.

| well hole | pumpjack | derrick | drill pipe |
|---|---|---|---|
| drill string | drill collar | drill bit | ~~oil field~~ |

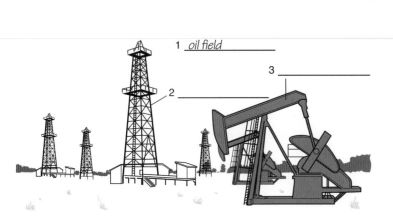

1 _oil field_

3 _____

2 _____

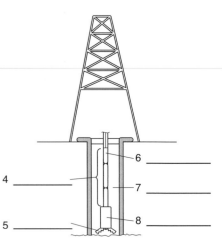

4 _____

5 _____

6 _____

7 _____

8 _____

**Speaking** 3 Practise in pairs. Look at the diagrams. Ask and answer questions.

A: *What's this?*
B: *It's a drill pipe. What are those?*
A: *Those are derricks.*

# Operating equipment

**1** Look at the pictures on the left. Then look at the photo on the right. What can you name?

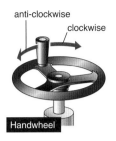

Handwheel

anti-clockwise clockwise

Flange

Handle

Gauge

Valve

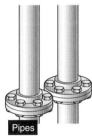

Pipes

**Listening** **2** 🔊 24 Listen to and read the conversation.

**Supervisor:**
OK. Listen carefully.
First, you turn this handwheel.
No, anti-clockwise.
Turn it until it's open.
Next, close this valve.
And then wait a couple of minutes.
Then read the gauge and write the pressure
   in the log book.
And finally, check the flanges and the valves.
Yes, that's right.

**Trainee:**
Understood.
Clockwise?
OK, anti-clockwise.
OK. Until it's open.
OK. Then close the valve.
Wait a couple of minutes.

OK. Got that.
For leaks?

**3** Match the verbs 1–5 with the nouns a–e.

| | | | |
|---|---|---|---|
| 1 | Turn | a) | the gauge |
| 2 | Close | b) | the pressure |
| 3 | Read | c) | the valve |
| 4 | Write | d) | the wheel |
| 5 | Check | e) | the flanges |

**Speaking** **4** Work in pairs. Student A turn to page 68. Student B turn to page 79.

**5** Now compare your notes with others in the class.

# Control panels

**1** Look at the picture and read the description.

> Look at this control panel. There's a start button top left. There's a stop button bottom right. The pressure gauge is in the middle. There's a warning lamp top right and the on/off switch is bottom left.

### Language

| There is / There are | |
|---|---|
| We use **there is / there are** to say something or somebody exists. | **There is / There's** a lamp on the panel. |
| | **There are** three lamps on the panel. |
| In the plural negative form we use *any*, not a number. | **There isn't (is not)** a switch. |
| | **There aren't (are not)** any switches. |
| In questions we use *any*, not a number. In short answers we omit the noun. | A: **Is there** a start button? |
| | B: Yes, **there is.** / No, **there isn't (is not).** |
| | A: **Are there** any buttons? |
| | B: Yes, **there are.** / No, **there aren't (are not).** |

**2** Now look at this control panel. Write a description like the one above.

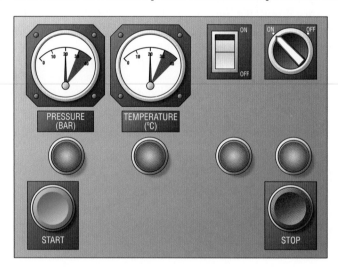

**Speaking** **3** Work in pairs. First draw a control panel. Put the controls where you like. Then describe it for your partner to draw.

# Telling the time

**Vocabulary**   **1**   🎵 **25**   Listen and repeat the times.

a) three    b) three fifteen    c) four thirty    d) five forty    e) six forty-five    f) seven fifty
o'clock

**2**   🎵 **26**   Listen and tick the times you hear.

□      ✓      □      □      □      □

**3**   🎵 **27**   Listen and write down the times you hear.

1  *Six o'clock*
2  _____
3  _____ , _____
4  _____ , _____
5  _____ , _____

**Listening**   **4**   🎵 **28**   Look at the departures board. Listen to the conversation.

**Speaking**   Practise in pairs. Ask and answer questions about other flights.

A: What time does the
    flight to Los Angeles
    depart/leave?
B: At seven thirty-five.
A: What's the flight
    number?
B: TH3946.
A: What's the gate?
B: A1.
A: Is it on time?
B: Yes, it is. / No, it isn't.
    It's delayed / cancelled.
A: Thank you. / Thanks.

**DEPARTURES**

| TIME | TO | FLIGHT NO. | GATE | REMARKS |
|---|---|---|---|---|
| 07:35 | LOS ANGELES | TH3946 | A1 | ON TIME |
| 07:40 | FRANKFURT | LN3211 | C3 | ON TIME |
| 07:45 | TORONTO | GT4638 | A2 | ON TIME |
| 07:45 | LONDON | HV3323 | B4 | DELAYED |
| 07:50 | NEW YORK | FD2753 | A6 | DELAYED |
| 07:55 | SYDNEY | LV2317 | A5 | ON TIME |
| 08:05 | PARIS | BD9032 | B1 | ON TIME |
| 08:15 | OSLO | F65610 | C4 | ON TIME |
| 08:20 | BUENOS AIRES | NB7792 | A4 | DELAYED |
| 08:25 | BARCELONE | GC5433 | C1 | ON TIME |
| 08:35 | TOKYO | LY4488 | B2 | ON TIME |
| 08:40 | MOSKOW | HF3280 | B4 | CANCELLED |
| 08:50 | ZURICH | TH7252 | A4 | ON TIME |
| 08:55 | MIAMI | LX3100 | A2 | ON TIME |
| 09:05 | HONG KONG | EN4267 | C4 | ON TIME |
| 09:10 | ROME | RZ1408 | B3 | DELAYED |
| 09:15 | HONOLULU | EK4319 | A1 | ON TIME |

# Asking questions about equipment

Listening **1**  ▶ 🎧 **29**  Listen and complete the sentences.

1  A: What's this?
   B: It's a pressure _gauge_____ .

2  A: What's this for?
   B: It's for checking the _____ .

3  A: What does this switch do?
   B: It starts the _____ .

4  A: How do I increase the speed?
   B: You _____ the dial.

5  A: How do I lower the pressure?
   B: You open the _____ .

6  A: What's this thing for?
   B: That's the power _____ . It starts the motor.

7  A: Did you say turn the handle?
   B: Yes, that's right.
   A: Clockwise or _____-clockwise?
   B: Clockwise.

8  A: What do I do next?
   B: Press the start _____ .
   A: OK.

**2**  ▶ 🎧 **30**  Write the words in the correct order. Listen to check.

1  What's for this ?
2  Did you the press say button ?
3  What's gauge for this ?
4  Did you pull say lever the ?
5  What this does switch do ?
6  Is this button a start ?
7  Does this thing motor the start ?

Speaking **3**  Practise in pairs. Use these pictures. Ask and answer questions.

A: *What's this? / What are these?*
B: *It's a helmet. / They're gloves.*
A: *What's this for? / What are these for?*
B: *It's for protecting your head. / They're for protecting your hands.*

# Health and safety: Warning signs

**Reading** 1 Here are some PPE signs. Match the instructions to the pictures.

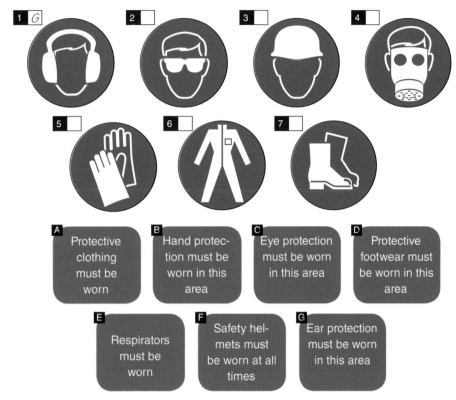

**Language**

| *must / mustn't* | |
|---|---|
| We use **must** or **mustn't** + infinitive for instructions that are compulsory. | *You **must** wear a helmet.* |
| | *You **mustn't** (**must not**) smoke here.* |

2 Write warnings using *must* or *mustn't*.

1 <u>You must turn off your phone.</u>
2 <u>You mustn't use your phone.</u>

**Speaking** 3 Practise in pairs. Ask and answer questions about the signs.

A: *What does this sign mean?*
B: *It means you must / mustn't … .*

# Making conversation

**31** Complete the conversations with the words in the box. Then listen to check.

| please | ~~Cantarell~~ | room | flask | idea | Kuwait | valve | ask |
|---|---|---|---|---|---|---|---|

**Conversation 1**
A: Where's _Cantarell_____ ?
B: I think it's in Mexico.
A: Oh yes, thank you.
B: No problem.

**Conversation 2**
A: Where's Greater Burgan?
B: I'm sure it's in _____ .
A: Oh, OK.

**Conversation 3**
A: I think the pressure's too high.
B: Oh, yes, you're right. Open the _____ .
A: OK. Good idea.

**Conversation 4**
A: I think the temperature's too high.
B: I don't think you're right. 200 degrees is OK.
A: Are you sure?
B: OK, go and _____ Jim.
A: OK. Will do.

**Conversation 5**
A: Where's your hard hat?
B: In my _____ . Why?
A: Go and get it. You must wear a hard hat in this area.
B: Oh, OK. I didn't know that. Sorry.

**Conversation 6**
A: Cup of tea?
B: Good _____ .
A: Milk and sugar?
B: Yes, _____ .

**Conversation 7**
A: Don't touch the _____ .
B: Why? Is it yours?
A: No, it's Norman's.
B: Oh, fair enough.

Speaking 2 Practise in pairs. Use all these phrases to make a conversation. Practise your conversation and then present it to the class.

| | |
|---|---|
| *Cup of tea?* | *Where's ...?* |
| *No problem.* | *Oh, OK.* |
| *OK. Good idea.* | *Are you sure?* |
| *OK. Will do.* | *I didn't know that. Sorry.* |
| *Good idea.* | *Fair enough.* |

# Review

**1** Complete the puzzle. What do the missing letters spell?

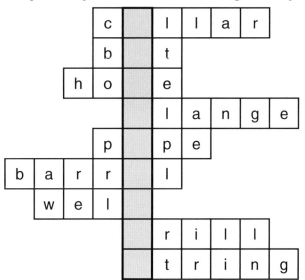

**2** Write down five different items in an oil field.

*pumpjack, ...*

**3** Write down three things you find on a control panel.

*switches,...*

**4** Write these times in words.

1 3:25 _____     4 2:10 _____

2 6:40 _____     5 7:45 _____

3 7:20 _____

**5** Look at these signs. Write what they mean.

1  *You must wear a helmet.*

- Talk about drilling a well
- Name common hand tools
- Ask for and give directions
- Understand helicopter safety intructions
- Order food in the canteen

# Drilling a well

**Listening** **1** ▶ 🎧 32 Look at the diagrams. Listen to the instructions about how to drill for oil.

1 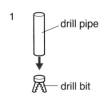 drill pipe / drill bit

2  drill collar

3 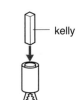 kelly

4 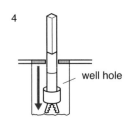 well hole

5 turntable

6 POWER / ON

7

8

9 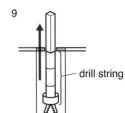 drill string

10 casing

**2** ▶ 🎧 32 Write the correct number next to each verb. Listen again to check.

*trip into = lower into*
*trip out of*
*= raise out of*

a) fix _____
b) install _____
c) drill _____
d) trip into _____
e) slide _____
f) trip out of _____
g) attach ___1___
h) put _____
i) turn on _____
j) attach _____

**Language**

| Sequencing | |
|---|---|
| We often put **sequencing words** at the beginning of a sentence. | *First*, attach the drill pipe to the drill bit. |
| | *Second* put the collar on the drill bit. |
| | *Then / After that / Next* drill the hole. |
| | *Finally*, install the casing in the well hole. |

**3** Practise in pairs. Give instructions about how to drill for oil. Use the diagrams to help you.

*First, attach the drill pipe to the drill bit. Second, ...*

# The rotary system

**Listening** 1   33   Listen and complete the sentences with words from the diagrams. Listen again to check.

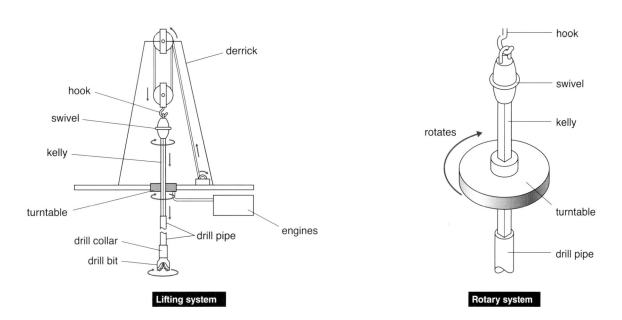

**Lifting system**        **Rotary system**

1 The _swivel_____ hangs from a hook.
2 The _____ connects the swivel to the drill pipe.
3 The kelly goes through the _____ .
4 The _____ turn the turntable.
5 The turntable _____ .
6 The turntable turns the _____ .
7 The kelly turns the _____ pipe.

2 Are these sentences true (T) or false (F)? Correct the false statements.

  1 The turntable rotates. T/F
  2 The kelly rotates. T/F
  3 The swivel rotates. T/F
  4 The hook rotates. T/F
  5 The drill pipe rotates. T/F
  6 The engines turn the turntable. T/F
  7 The turntable turns the kelly. T/F
  8 The kelly turns the turntable. T/F
  9 The kelly turns the drill pipe. T/F
10 The drill pipe turns the kelly. T/F
11 The hook connects the swivel to the drill pipe. T/F
12 The kelly connects the swivel to the drill pipe. T/F
13 The swivel connects the hook to the kelly. T/F
14 The kelly connects the drill pipe to the swivel. T/F
15 The drill pipe connects the kelly to the turntable. T/F

**Speaking** 3 Work in pairs. Close your books. Draw a diagram of the rotary system. Explain how it works to a partner.

*A: How does the rotary system work?*
*B: Well, the ... .*

# Lifting gear

**1** Read the text. Underline the words from the diagram.

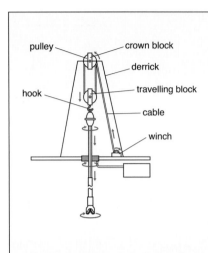

pulley — crown block
— derrick
hook — travelling block
— cable
— winch

There are two <u>blocks</u>. Both blocks use pulleys. The cable goes from the winch to the blocks. The crown block does not move. It is fixed to the top of the derrick. The travelling block hangs from the crown block. It moves up and down. The winch pulls or releases the cable. When it pulls the cable, the travelling block goes up. When it releases the cable, the travelling block goes down.

**2** Complete these sentences.

1 The cable _goes from the winch to the blocks_____ .
2 The crown block _____ .
3 The travelling block _____ .
4 The winch _____ .
5 When the winch pulls the cable, the travelling block _____
_____ .
6 When the winch releases the cable, the travelling block _____
_____ .

**Speaking** **3** Look at these pictures. Describe the pictures using these phrases.

*This is a …*
*This goes from … to …*
*This does not …*
*This pulls the …*
*When the …, the …*

# Hand tools

**Vocabulary**  **1**  Match the pictures like this.

*The paint brush and the paint go together.*

Paint brush | Drill | Screwdriver | Pliers | Wrench | Hammer

Screw | Nut | Paint | Wire | Nail | Hole

**Listening**  **2**  🔊 34  Listen to three conversations and match them to the pictures.

Conversation 1 _____

Conversation 2 _____

Conversation 3 _____

A   B 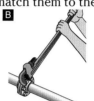  C

**Language**

### to / too

| | |
|---|---|
| The words **to** and **too** have different meanings. | *The nut is **too** small.* |
| | *Listen **to** the instructions.* |
| | *We need a wrench **to** do this.* |
| | *They're next **to** the flask.* |
| | *Go from the canteen **to** the washroom.* |

**3**  Complete the following sentences with *to* or *too*.

1  This hammer is __*too*__ small.
2  The wrench is next _____ the toolbox.
3  We use computers _____ record the data.
4  Count from one _____ ten.
5  This screwdriver is _____ big.

**Vocabulary**  **4**  Match the words.

1  pipe                 a)  paint
2  electric            b)  hammer
3  reflective        c)  wrench
4  needle-nose      d)  pliers
5  sledge           e)  screwdriver

**Speaking**  **5**  Practise in pairs. Talk about problems you can have with the items on this page.

# Directions

**1**  🔊 35  Listen to these directions. Complete the sentences.

Where's the supervisor's office?
1  It's at the end _of_ _____ the corridor.
2  It's down the corridor, _____ the right.
3  It's along the corridor, third door _____ the left.
4  It's _____ the door.

Where's the car park?
5  Go _____ the gate. The car park is on the left.
6  Drive _____ the trees. It's on the right.
7  It's _____ the derrick.
8  It's _____ the pumpjack.
9  It's _____ the derrick and the pumpjack.

**2**  Look at the map. You are at A. Read these directions for the route to the temporary safe refuge (TSR) on an oil platform. Draw the route on the map.

Escape routes on an oil platform

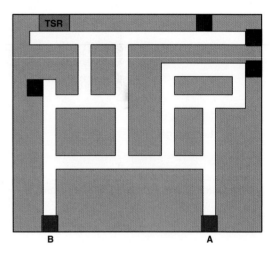

> Go straight ahead. Take the first turning on your left and go straight ahead. Take the second turning on your right. Go straight until you come to a T-junction. Turn left. The TSR is on your right.

**Writing**  **3**  Use the map above. Write directions for the route from B to the temporary safe refuge.

**Language**

| supervisors / supervisor's / supervisors' | |
|---|---|
| We add an *s* to make the noun plural. | *We have two supervisor**s** here, one for safety and one for technical control.* |
| **'s** and **s'** are used to show possession. The position of the apostrophe (') shows whether the noun is singular or plural. | *This is the supervisor**'s** office. (one supervisor)* |
| | *This is the supervisor**s'** office. (two or more supervisors)* |

**4**  Draw a map of your workplace. Practise directions in pairs. Say something about the places on your map.

*You must wear PPE in this area.*
*This is the supervisor's office.*
*Leave your phone at reception.*
*You mustn't smoke here.*

# Health and safety: Helicopters

**Listening** **1**   ▶ 🎧 36   Look at this picture. Then listen to and read the safety instructions. Complete the instructions.

Here are some instructions. First of all, remove any loose items which might blow away. Always approach a (1) _helicopter_____ where the pilot can see you. The tail (2) _____ is dangerous. Get in the helicopter only when the (3) _____ signals you to do so. Fasten your seatbelt as soon as you are seated and put on your ear protection. This flight is over water so you must wear a survival suit and a (4) _____ .

**Reading** **2**   Read the text again and answer these questions.

1. Who is in charge of the helicopter?
2. What do you put on your ears?
3. What must you remove?
4. What do you do when the pilot signals you?
5. What do you do with the seatbelt?
6. What must you wear for a flight over water?

**3**   Put the sentences in the correct order.

a) Remove loose items. ☐

b) Fasten your seatbelt. ☐

c) Get in the helicopter. ☐

d) Approach where the pilot can see you. ☐

e) Put on ear protection. ☐

f) Put on a survival suit and lifejacket. 1

g) Wait for the pilot's signal. ☐

**Speaking** **4**   Work in pairs. Student A turn to page 68. Student B turn to page 79.

# Off-shift in the canteen

**Vocabulary** **1** Match the words in the box to the pictures.

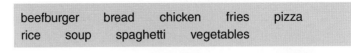

| beefburger | bread | chicken | fries | pizza |
| rice | soup | spaghetti | vegetables |

**Listening** **2** ▶ 37 Listen to three oil workers in a canteen. What do they order? How much does it cost?

| Food | Drink | Price |
|------|-------|-------|
|      |       |       |
|      |       |       |
|      |       |       |

**3** Listen again and look at the menu. What mistakes does the cashier make?

| Food | |
|------|------|
| chicken soup | $1.50 |
| vegetable soup | $1.50 |
| spaghetti | $6.00 |
| pizza | $7.35 |
| beefburger | $3.00 |
| cheeseburger | $3.50 |
| steak | $9.00 |
| fried egg | $0.50 |
| french fries | $0.50 |
| rice | $0.40 |
| extra mushrooms / onions / cheese | $0.50 |
| bread | $0.20 |
| **Drinks** | |
| tea | $0.50 |
| coffee | $0.75 |
| cola | $0.50 |
| orange juice | $0.50 |
| lemonade | $0.50 |
| water | free |

**Language**

| **Asking for and about food** | |
|---|---|
| There are different ways to ask for and about food. | *I'd like* a beefburger, please. |
| | *Could I have* some fries, please? |
| | *What's* that / this? |
| | A: *How about* a cup of tea?<br>B: That sounds good. |
| | A: *Would you like* a plate of spaghetti?<br>B: Yes, please. |

**Speaking** **4** Work in pairs. Student A turn to page 68. Student B turn to page 79.

# Review

**Writing**  **1** Write down the following.

1 three tools
2 three things to wear in a helicopter
3 three things to eat
4 three things to drink

**2** Label these diagrams. Then write five sentences about them. Use the words in the box to help you.

| turn | rotate | hang from | connect | go through | go from |

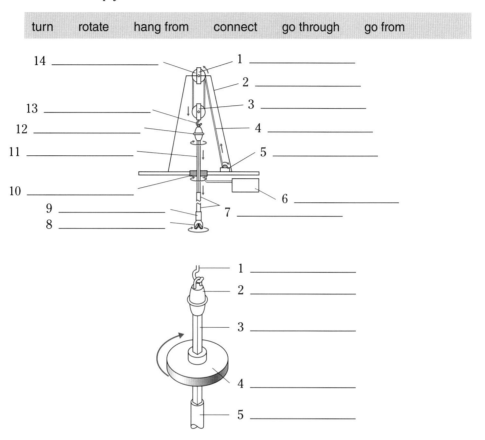

**3** Write down instructions to get from A to B.

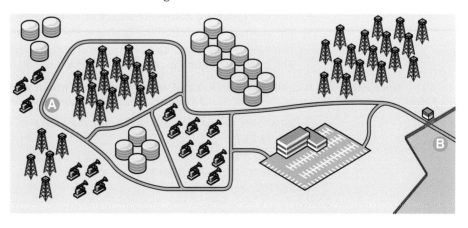

# Working offshore

- Describe oil rig systems
- Talk about dimensions
- Explain what a medic does
- Talk about basic medical problems
- Describe the crew quarters on an oil rig

## Oil rig systems

**Vocabulary** **1** Look at the diagram. Are these statements true (T) or false (F)?

1 The turntable is on the platform at the bottom of the derrick. T/F
2 The block and the hook are at the top of the derrick. T/F
3 The engines are below the platform. T/F
4 The pipe racks are to the left of the platform. T/F
5 The motor is above the generator. T/F
6 The water tank is to the right of the mud pit below the platform. T/F

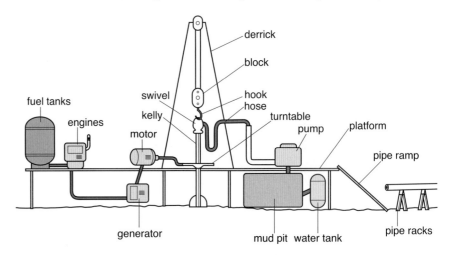

**2** Underline all the mistakes in these statements. Correct the mistakes.

1 The motor is <u>below</u> the platform, to the left of the engines. *above*
2 The fuel tanks are above the platform, to the right of the engines.
3 The ramp is to the left of the platform and to the right of the racks.
4 The mud pit is to the right of the pump and above the water tank.
5 The pump is below the platform, to the left of the derrick.

**Speaking** **3** Practise in pairs. Ask and answer questions about where things are on the oil rig.

A: *What's above the turntable and below the hook?*
B: *The swivel.*
A: *Correct! Now your turn.*
B: *Where is/are ... ? / What's ... ?*
A: *It's/They're/The ... .*

# What does it do?

**Listening** 1    🔊 38   Listen to and read the conversation.

    A: What's this?
    B: It's a derrick.
    A: What does it do?
    B: It supports the block.
    A: Did you say the block?
    B: Yes, that's correct.

2    🔊 39   Listen to and read the conversation.

    A: Does the motor turn the turntable?
    B: Yes, it does.
    A: And the engines? Do the engines provide the power?
    B: Yes, they do.
    A: Does the pump drive the generator?
    B: No, it doesn't. The engines drive the generator.
    A: Do the tanks on the left hold water?
    B: No, they don't. They hold fuel.

3    🔊 40   Complete the sentences. Then listen to check.

   1 The _engines_____ provide the power.
   2 The fuel _____ hold fuel for the engines.
   3 The engines drive the _____ .
   4 The generator provides electrical power for the _____ and the pump.
   5 The pump sucks mud from the mud _____ .
   6 The motor turns the _____ .
   7 The water tank _____ water for the mud pit.
   8 The mud pit contains the _____ fluid.
   9 The pipe racks support the _____ pipes.

**Speaking** 4 Practise in pairs. Ask and answer questions about what things do on the oil rig. Use the diagram on page 36.

    A: *What's this?*
    B: *What does it do?*
    A: *Does the … ?*
    B: *Do the … ?*
    A: *Did you say …?*

# Dimensions

**1**  🔊 41  Listen to and read the conversation.

A: How long is this pipe?
B: It's 30 feet long.
A: Did you say 30 feet?
B: Yes, that's correct.
A: What's that in metres?
B: About 10 metres.
A: OK. What's the diameter?
B: The outside diameter is 6 inches. The wall thickness is half an inch. And, before you ask, an inch is about two and a half centimetres. So that's about 15 centimetres outside diameter and a wall thickness of just over a centimetre.
A: So the bore is about 12.5 centimetres.
B: That's right.
A: OK, thank you.
B: You're welcome.

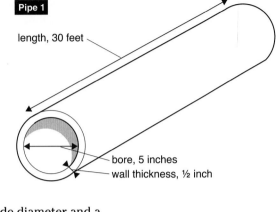

Pipe 1

length, 30 feet

bore, 5 inches

wall thickness, ½ inch

**2**  🔊 42  Listen and complete the sentences.

1  1 foot is equal to _____ inches.
2  1 inch is about _____ centimetres.
3  1 metre is about _____ feet.

**Speaking**  **3**  Work in pairs. Student A turn to page 68. Student B turn to page 79.

| Pipe | Length | Outside diameter | Wall thickness | Bore |
|------|--------|------------------|----------------|------|
| 2    |        |                  |                |      |
| 3    |        |                  |                |      |

# Offshore fixed platforms

**Reading**  **1**   Read the text and complete the dimensions on the diagram.

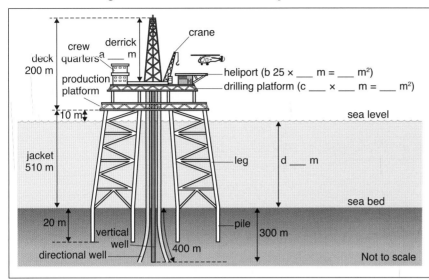

This offshore fixed platform is 710 metres high from the top of the derrick to the sea bed. The derrick is 100 metres high. The sea is 500 metres deep. The piles go 20 metres into the sea bed. The heliport on the right has an area of 500 square metres. The drilling platform is 40 metres long and 30 metres wide, so it has an area of 1200 square metres.

**2**   Write down the following information.

1. The height of the jacket above sea level
2. The height of the deck, including the derrick, above the jacket
3. The number of platforms
4. The height of the derrick above the drilling platform
5. The depth of the piles below the sea bed
6. The depth of the vertical well below the sea bed
7. The length of the directional well below the sea bed
8. The area of the drilling platform

**Writing**  **3**   Write the words in the correct order to make sentences.

1. pipeline kilometres is long The five .
2. five hundred is The deep sea metres .
3. wide The metres is heliport twenty-five .
4. metres The drilling platform the forty length of is .

**4**   Use these words to make sentences.

1. vertical well / deep
2. derrick / high
3. heliport / long / and / wide
4. piles / deep
5. drilling platform / long

**Language**

### Dimensions

| We can use a noun or the related adjective to talk about dimensions. | Adjective | Noun |
|---|---|---|
| | The pipe is 20 metres **long**. | The **length** of the pipe is 20 metres. |
| | The wall is half an inch **thick**. | The **thickness** of the wall is half an inch. |
| | The sea is 500 metres **deep**. | The **depth** of the sea is 500 metres. |
| | The heliport is 25 metres **wide**. | The **width** of the heliport is 25 metres. |
| | The derrick is 100 metres **high**. | The **height** of the derrick is 100 metres. |

**Speaking**  **5**   Practise in pairs. Use the diagram to talk about the dimensions of the platform.

# Asking for information

Language

## Asking about dimensions

| We use *How* + adjective + *is it?* to ask about dimensions using the adjective form of the word. | **How** long is it? |
| | **How** thick is it? |
| | **How** deep is it? |
| | **How** wide is it? |
| | **How** high is it? |
| We use *What is the* + noun? to ask about dimensions using the noun form of the word. | **What is** the length? |
| | **What is** the thickness? |
| | **What is** the depth? |
| | **What is** the width? |
| | **What is** the height? |

**1** Ask and answer questions about the offshore fixed platform. Use the words given and the diagram on page 39.

1 high / the top of the derrick / above sea level
2 area / heliport
3 deep / sea at the platform
4 width / drilling platform
5 height / jacket / above the sea bed

Language

## many / much

| We use **many** with nouns we can count. | How **many** barrels of oil does it produce? |
| | How **many** people are there in a crew? |
| We use **much** with nouns we cannot count. | How **much** oil do they have? |
| | How **much** fuel is in the tank? |

**2** ▶ 🔘 43 Complete this conversation using *much* and *many*. Listen to check.

A: Tell me about the platform. How (1) _much_ oil does it produce?
B: It produces about 21,000 barrels per day.
A: How (2) _____ tonnes is that per year?
B: Let me see. That's over one million tonnes per year.
A: How (3) _____ oil workers are there on the platform?
B: I think there are about 120.
A: How (4) _____ money do the oil workers earn?
B: They earn quite a lot because they have to work away from home.

Speaking **3** Practise in pairs. Ask and answer more questions about the offshore fixed platform.

# Health and safety: In the sick bay

**Reading**  **1**  Read the text. What do medics do? Make a list.

Every rig has a doctor or a medic. Their job is to look after any medical problems on the rig. Normally they treat patients in the sick bay. Sometimes they send patients to hospital by helicopter. Medical staff can have other jobs, too. They check water supplies. They inspect food. They order medical supplies. They also train workers in first aid.

**Listening**  **2**  **🔊 44**  Listen to the conversations. What three questions does the medic ask?

**3**  **🔊 44**  Listen again. Write down the six medical problems you hear.

1  _cough_
2  sun_____
3  head_____
4  I hurt my _____ .
5  I've got something in my _____ .
6  I hurt my _____ .

**4**  **🔊 44**  Listen again. Write down the solution.

1  cough _medicine_
2  sun _____
3  _____
4  _____ in the other room
5  eye _____
6  X-_____

**Language**

### have / have got

| We use **have got** instead of **have** in informal British English. American English does not use **have got**. | I **have** a headache. | I**'ve got** a headache. |
|---|---|---|
| | He **has** sunburn. | He**'s got** sunburn. |
| | We both **have** this cough. | We**'ve** both **got** this cough. |

**5**  Practise in pairs. One of you is a medic, the other a patient. Make similar conversations to those you heard.

A:  What's the matter / problem?
B:  I have / I've got … .

# Crew quarters

**1** Read the text.

The crew quarters are on two levels. The upper level houses the galley, the mess area, the recreation room, the tool pusher's office and quarters and the company man's office and quarters.

The lower level has the crew changing areas, showers and toilets, a fitness room, washing machines, crew lockers, crew cabins and the first aid room and sick bay.

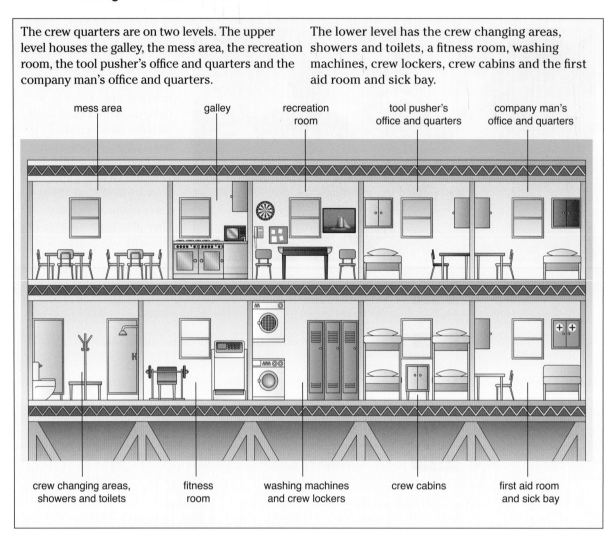

mess area · galley · recreation room · tool pusher's office and quarters · company man's office and quarters

crew changing areas, showers and toilets · fitness room · washing machines and crew lockers · crew cabins · first aid room and sick bay

**Listening** **2** 🔊 45 Complete the sentences. Then listen to check.

1 OK, the _recreation_ room. There's a TV, a snooker table, a telephone and some books. There's also a notice board.
2 The _____ area? Just tables and chairs and a window to the galley.
3 The _____ ? It's a kitchen. It's where we cook our food.
4 The _____ room? We have a running machine and some other sports equipment.
5 The _____ machines are on all the time. We get very dirty in this job.
6 Everyone has a _____ . That's where we keep our PPE.

**Speaking** **3** Draw a plan of the crew quarters on an oil rig. Draw two levels. Explain your plan to a partner but do not show your partner your drawing. Your partner draws your plan.

# Review

**Writing**

**1**  Write five sentences about this diagram.

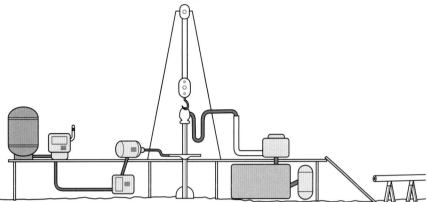

*Example: The engines provide the power. They are to the right of the fuel tanks.*

**2**  Write three sentences to describe this pipe.

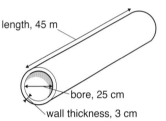

length, 45 m

bore, 25 cm

wall thickness, 3 cm

*This pipe is 45 metres …*

**3**  Complete this text.

A typical offshore fixed platform is 710 metres high from the top of the derrick to the (1) _____ . The derrick is 100 metres high. The sea is 500 metres (2) _____ . The piles go 20 metres into the sea (3) _____ . The heliport on the right has an (4) _____ of 500 square metres. The drilling platform is 40 metres long and 30 metres (5) _____ , so it has an area of 1200 square metres.

**4**  Complete these sentences with *much* or *many*.

1  How _____ people work on the rig?
2  How _____ oil does the rig produce?
3  How _____ barrels of oil does the rig produce?
4  How _____ tables are there in the galley?
5  How _____ money do the oil workers earn?

**5**  What does a medic on an oil rig do? Write three sentences.

*Example: A medic treats patients.*

**6**  Write seven words to complete the word spider.

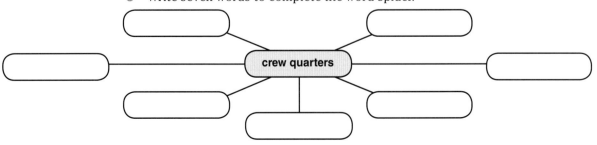

crew quarters

# 6 Refining

- Talk about refineries
- Talk about refinery jobs
- Use colours
- Talk about days, months and dates
- Talk about emergency procedures
- Talk about the weather

## Refineries

Substation

Hazmat area

Main gate

**Reading** 1 Read this text.

> Refineries change crude oil into different petroleum products. There
> are three main processes. First the crude oil is separated into different
> components. Then the components are converted using heat and pressure.
> Lastly, chemicals are added to make the final products. The control room
> is the centre of the refinery. Electrical power is provided by the substation.
> Hazardous materials are stored in the hazmat area.

**Listening** 2 🔊 46 Listen to six visitors at the main gate to a refinery. Complete the table.

| Visitor | Time | Name of visitor | Reason for visit | Where |
|---------|------|-----------------|------------------|-------|
| 1 | | Hans Clements | Meeting with Dr Schmidt | |
| 2 | | Abdullah Al-Rakhis | | Hazmat area |
| 3 | | Sally Digby | New employee | |
| 4 | | Marisa Codreanu and Dennis Poljakovic | | Separation area |
| 5 | | | Delivery of spare parts | Control room |
| 6 | | Connie Grieve | | Substation |

**Speaking** 3 Practise in pairs. Have conversations like the ones you heard. Use these
phrases and sentences.

*Good morning/afternoon.*　　*I'm here to see … .*
*Could I see your ID, please?*　*One moment, please.*
*Thank you.*

# Parts of a refinery

**Vocabulary** 1 Match the words 1–13 with their descriptions a–m.

1 substation
2 conversion area
3 tank farm
4 canteen
5 main gate
6 administration building
7 separation area

8 river
9 treatment area
10 labs

11 parking area
12 hazardous materials area
13 control room

a) water supply for chemical processes
b) the centre of the refinery
c) control of access
d) space for cars
e) electricity supply
f) store of dangerous materials
g) where chemicals are added to make products ready for market
h) a place to get food
i) offices
j) storage tanks for different petroleum products
k) the location of the distillation columns
l) the location of the labs
m) where heat and pressure are used to change the components

**Listening** 2 🔊 47 Listen to the information about a refinery. Answer these questions.

1 How big is the refinery?
2 How many gates does it have?
3 How many parking areas does it have?
4 What is the substation for?
5 What is the river for?
6 Where are the distillation columns?
7 What are the buildings in the treatment area?

**Vocabulary** 3 Look at the picture. Which parts of the refinery can you see?

**Speaking** 4 Work in pairs. Draw a map of a refinery. Explain the different areas to a visitor.

*This is the admin building.*
*These are our offices.*
*This is the substation.*
*This provides power for the refinery.*

# Refinery jobs

**Reading**  **1**  Read the texts. Match the jobs in the box to the descriptions.

> safety instructor  ~~control room operator~~  maintenance supervisor
> pump system operator  lab technician

1 My job is to work in the refinery control room. I monitor equipment and troubleshoot problems.  *control room operator*
2 I'm responsible for all the pump systems in the refinery. I use different instruments in my work, including pressure gauges and flowmeters.
3 I work in a lab. My job is to add chemicals to the products and carry out tests. I write a lot of reports.
4 My job is to co-ordinate and supervise a team of engineers and technicians. Together we inspect and maintain refinery equipment and piping systems. Sometimes we repair equipment.
5 I train all the employees in everything to do with fire safety. This includes hazmat training as well as emergency procedures.

**2**  Find the odd one out. Explain why.
1 employee, engineer, equipment, technician, supervisor
2 pressure gauge, piping systems, pump systems, flowmeters, training
3 fire safety, write reports, carry out tests, monitor equipment, train employees

**3**  Underline the following word partnerships in the descriptions above.
a) refinery equipment
b) fire safety
c) emergency procedures
d) piping systems
e) hazmat training
f) pressure gauges

**4**  Find verbs in the texts above which go with these nouns.
1 employees  *co-ordinate*
2 equipment
3 reports
4 problems
5 instruments

**Speaking**  **5**  Describe a job to a partner. Your partner has to guess the job you are describing.

# In the control room: PCBs and resistors

**Reading**   **1**   Read this explanation of PCBs.

> **PCBs**
> Refinery control rooms contain a lot of complex electrical equipment.
> Technicians look after this equipment. Sometimes technicians repair printed
> circuit boards, or PCBs.
>
>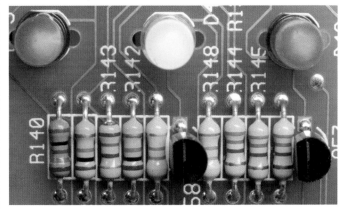
>
> Look at the resistors on this PCB.
>
>
>
> The colour bands show the value of the resistor in ohms
> ($\Omega$). Ten different colours represent the numbers 0 to 9.
> The first two bands are the first two digits of the resistance.
> The third band is the multiplier.
> The multiplier tells you the number of zeroes to add after
> the first two digits.
> The final band is the tolerance.
> On the resistor shown above, orange = 3, orange = 3,
> black = 0, so the resistance is 33 $\Omega$.
>
> | | |
> |---|---|
> | black | 0 |
> | brown | 1 |
> | red | 2 |
> | orange | 3 |
> | yellow | 4 |
> | green | 5 |
> | blue | 6 |
> | purple | 7 |
> | grey | 8 |
> | white | 9 |

**2**   Answer these questions.

   1   What does PCB stand for?
   2   What do the colour bands on the resistors show?
   3   What do the first two bands mean?
   4   What does the third band tell you?
   5   What is the fourth band for?

**Speaking**   **3**   Work in pairs. Tell your partner the colours of the first three bands of a resistor.
They work out the resistance.

   A: *My colours are purple, then green, then black.*
   B: *OK, so that's 75 $\Omega$.*
   A: *Correct! Now your turn.*
   B: *OK. My colours are yellow, purple and red.*
   A: *That's 4700 $\Omega$ or 4.7 k$\Omega$.*

# Dates

**1**   [▶ 48]   Listen to two short conversations. Tick the days you hear.

| | | | |
|---|---|---|---|
| Monday | ☐ | Friday | ☐ |
| Tuesday | ☐ | Saturday | ☐ |
| Wednesday | ☐ | Sunday | ☐ |
| Thursday | ☐ | | |

**2**   [▶ 49]   Listen and repeat the months of the year. Mark the stress.

| | | |
|---|---|---|
| January | February | March |
| April | May | June |
| July | August | September |
| October | November | December |

**Writing**   **3**   What comes next?

1   Monday, Tuesday, Wednesday, *Thursday* _____
2   Saturday, Monday, Wednesday, _____
3   January, March, May, _____
4   December, November, October, _____
5   March, June, September, _____

**Language**

---

**Dates**

We say *the first of January, the second of February, the third of March*, etc. or *January the first*.

| | | |
|---|---|---|
| 1st = first | 11th = eleventh | 21st = twenty-first |
| 2nd = second | 12th = twelfth | 22nd = twenty-second |
| 3rd = third | 13th = thirteenth | 23rd = twenty-third |
| 4th = fourth | 14th = fourteenth | 24th = twenty-fourth |
| 5th = fifth | 15th = fifteenth | 25th = twenty-fifth |
| 6th = sixth | 16th = sixteenth | 26th = twenty-sixth |
| 7th = seventh | 17th = seventeenth | 27th = twenty-seventh |
| 8th = eighth | 18th = eighteenth | 28th = twenty-eighth |
| 9th = ninth | 19th = nineteenth | 29th = twenty-ninth |
| 10th = tenth | 20th = twentieth | 30th = thirtieth |
| | | 31st = thirty-first |

---

**4**   Dictate days and months to your partner.

**5**   Practise in pairs. Ask and answer questions. Find a new partner and repeat.

| | |
|---|---|
| *What day is it today/tomorrow?* | *It's Tuesday.* |
| *What month is it?* | *It's December.* |
| *What's the date today?* | *It's the third of February.* |
| *When's your birthday?* | *It's on the fourteenth of July.* |

# Health and safety: Emergency procedures

**Reading**  1  Read these emergency procedures. Why do you walk upwind?

## Emergency procedures

1  **Raise the alarm.**
2  **Contact the emergency services.**
3  **Switch off all machinery.**
4  **Proceed upwind to an assembly area.**
5  **Check that all your crew or department are present or accounted for.**
6  **Report to the senior person present.**

**Listening**  2  🔊 50  Listen to a supervisor talking about emergency procedures. Does he forget anything?

3  Match these actions to the procedures above.
   a) telephone
   b) talk
   c) break glass   *1*
   d) push stop button
   e) walk
   f) count heads

4  Match these sentences to the procedures above.
   a) I would like to report a fire in the administration building.
   b) My crew are all present or accounted for.
   c) Does anyone know where John is?
   d) Follow me.
   e) Turn off the generator.
   f) Fire! Fire! Fire!   *1*

**Speaking**  5  Work in pairs. Student A turn to page 68. Student B turn to page 79.

# Talking about the weather

Listening **1**   ▶ 🔊 **51**   Listen and read.

     1   It's raining.
     2   It's windy.
     3   It's a storm. Listen to the thunder.

**2**   🔊 **52**   Listen and complete the table.

| –20° C | 0° C | 20° C | 40° C |
|---|---|---|---|
| It's very _____ today. | It's freezing. | It's a nice day. | It's very hot today. |
| It's twenty below and … | It's _____ degrees. | It's 20 degrees. | It's _____ degrees. |
| … it's snowing. | There's ice on the roads. | No _____ today. | It's very windy. |

Speaking **3**   Practise in pairs. Discuss the weather report with your partner.

| Place | Today | | Tomorrow | |
|---|---|---|---|---|
| Aberdeen | –10° C | ☁❄ | 3° C | 🌧 |
| Los Angeles | 32° C | ☀ | 33° C | ☀ |
| Moscow | –20° C | ☁❄ | –23° C | ☁❄ |
| Rio de Janeiro | 28° C | ☁ | 25° C | ☀ |
| Riyadh | 45° C | ☀ | 45° C | ☀ |
| Sydney | 18° C | ☁ | 21° C | ☀ |

| Celsius | Fahrenheit |
|---|---|
| –30 | –22 |
| –25 | –13 |
| –20 | –4 |
| –15 | 5 |
| –10 | 14 |
| –5 | 23 |
| 0 | 32 |
| 5 | 41 |
| 10 | 50 |
| 15 | 59 |
| 20 | 68 |
| 25 | 77 |
| 30 | 86 |
| 35 | 95 |
| 40 | 104 |
| 45 | 113 |

A: *What's the weather like in Aberdeen today?*
B: *Freezing. It's minus 10.*
A: *And tomorrow?*
B: *It's going to be 3 degrees and raining.*
A: *What about Riyadh?*
B: *It's hot. 45 degrees.*
A: *What's that in Fahrenheit?*
B: *A hundred and thirteen degrees.*

# Review

**Writing**

**1**  What does a refinery do? Write three sentences.

**2**  Look at the audioscript for track 47 on page 75. Write questions to get these answers.

1   It's nearly 3 km long and 1 km wide.
    *Example: How big is the refinery?*
2   Three.
3   Electrical power.
4   From the river.
5   In the separation area.

**3**  Write a sentence about what each of these people do.

1   control room operator
2   safety instructor
3   maintenance supervisor
4   pump system operator
5   lab technician

**4**  Complete the emergency procedures for a refinery.

1   Raise _____ .
2   Contact _____ .
3   Switch _____ .
4   Proceed _____ .
5   Check _____ .
6   Report _____ .

**5**  Complete each of these word spiders.

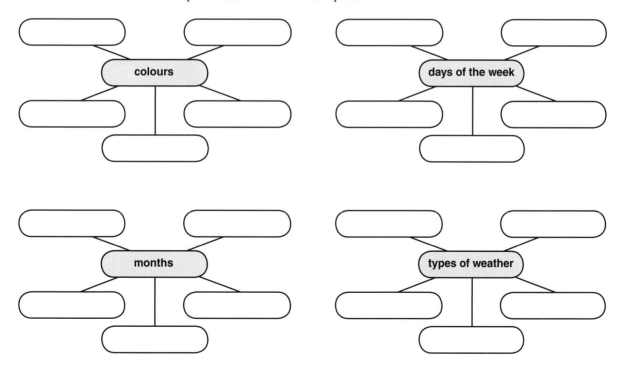

colours

days of the week

months

types of weather

## 7 Storage

- Talk about petroleum products
- Describe storage facilities
- Explain how to operate a fire extinguisher
- Talk about past incidents
- Request items from the storeroom

## Petroleum products

**Listening** **1** ▶ 🔊 **53** Listen to the descriptions of five different oil depots. As you listen, tick the petroleum products you hear.

1  asphalt     ☑    7  petrochemicals (feedstock)  ☐
2  diesel fuels  ☐    8  paraffin wax  ☐
3  jet fuel  ☐    9  automotive and industrial lubricants  ☐
4  kerosene  ☐    10  liquefied petroleum gas  ☐
5  gasoline  ☐    11  propane  ☐
6  fuel oils  ☐    12  butane  ☐

**Vocabulary** **2** Match the words to the pictures.

1  catwalk  *E*
2  tank farm
3  bullet tank
4  underground tank
5  road tanker

**3** You have one minute. Close your book. Write down as many petroleum products as you can. Compare your list with others in the class.

52    **7** Storage

# Properties

**Reading** 1 Complete the text with the headings in the box.

| Plastics | Jet fuel | Synthetic rubber | Petrol |

**Petroleum products**

1 _____

Also called gasoline, this is a liquid fuel for vehicles on land and sea. It ignites easily in engines. It remains liquid at normal temperatures.

2 _____

This is a liquid fuel for aircraft and rockets. It remains liquid at very low temperatures.

3 _____

Also called polymers, these are usually light and strong and do not rust. They can be made into different shapes. There are two types.

- Thermoplastics: When you heat thermoplastics, they melt and you can shape them. You can reheat them and melt them again and again. This means that you can recycle them. Water bottles are made of thermoplastics.
- Thermosets: You cannot re-melt thermosets. They are heat-resistant. Engine parts are sometimes made of thermosets.

Synthetic fibres are made from plastics. Nylon is one example. Synthetic fibres are often water-resistant and do not stretch or break when you pull them. They are used to make ropes.

4 _____

This is a heat-resistant and corrosion-resistant material. Oil and petrol cannot damage it. For this reason, it is often used to make fuel hoses.

2 Match the sentences to the pictures.

1 Metal rusts.  *B*
2 Rubber stretches.
3 Warning: corrosive materials.

4 This jacket is water-resistant.
5 Ice melts at room temperature.

A
B
C
D
E

3 Complete the sentences with words from the text above.

1 Fire hoses are made from *rubber* _____ .
2 _____ is used in aircraft.
3 Car fuel is called _____ or _____ .
4 _____ is a synthetic fibre.
5 Water bottles are made of _____ .

4 Match the products 1–5 with their descriptions a–e.

1 petrol
2 jet fuel
3 thermosets
4 synthetic fibres
5 synthetic rubber

a) cannot be re-melted
b) corrosion-resistant
c) remains liquid at low temperatures
d) do not stretch when pulled
e) ignites easily

**Speaking** 5 Practise in pairs. Describe a petroleum product but do not name it. Your partner has to guess what it is.

A: *This product is black. You drive on it.*
A: *No. It's in the road.*
A: *Yes.*

B: *Is it a tyre?*
B: *Is it asphalt?*

# Describing storage facilities

**1** Read the text. Are these sentences true (T) or false (F)? Correct the false statements.

1 The <u>smallest</u> tank we have is 34,000 gallons. T/F̶  *largest*
2 The longest bullet tank is 18 metres. T/F
3 The pressure in the bullet tanks is lower than in the fuel oil tanks. T/F
4 The nearest rig is 45 kilometres away. T/F

This facility is **bigger** than our others. In fact, it is the **biggest** facility we have. These tanks are for kerosene. They are much **smaller** than the tanks we use for the other fuel oils. The **largest** tank we have is 34,000 gallons. Here it is on the right. Here you can see the bullet tanks, which we use for LPG. The **longest** we have is 18 metres. The **shortest** is 6 metres. The pressure in the LPG tanks is normally around 5 bar. This is much **higher** than in the fuel oil tanks. Propane and butane are both **heavier** than air, so leaks can be a problem. The gas does not go away. The refinery is not **far**, only 3 kilometres from here. The **closest** rig is 35 kilometres away. The **furthest** is 150 kilometres.

## Language

### Comparing things

| We use an **adjective** to describe a noun. | This is a **big** facility. |
|---|---|
| We use a **comparative** to compare two things. | This facility is **bigger** than our others. |
| We use a **superlative** to compare three or more things. | This is the **biggest** facility we have. |

| Short adjectives | close | closer | the closest |
|---|---|---|---|
|  | great | greater | the greatest |
| Adjectives ending in -y | heavy | heavier | the heaviest |
|  | easy | easier | the easiest |
| Long adjectives | important | more/less important | the most/least important |
| Irregular adjectives | good | better | the best |
|  | bad | worse | the worst |
|  | far | further | the furthest |

**2** Read the information about the three storage facilities. Then complete the sentences.

| | Al Gabar Oil Depot | Yakunst Tank Farm | Hangdong Terminal |
|---|---|---|---|
| Built | 1962 | 1998 | 2001 |
| Distance to refinery | 3 km | 120 km | 27 km |
| Capacity | 33 million litres | 32 million litres | 54 million litres |
| Number of tanks | 27 | 44 | 60 |

1 Al Gabar is _older_____ (old) than Yakunst.
2 Al Gabar is _____ (old) depot in the table.
3 Yakunst is _____ (far) from a refinery.
4 Al Gabar is _____ (close) to a refinery than Hangdong.
5 Hangdong has _____ (large) storage capacity.
6 Hangdong has _____ (great) number of tanks.

**Writing** **3** Write five more sentences comparing the three facilities.

**Speaking** **4** Compare your sentences with others in the class.

# Health and safety: Fire safety

**1**   ▶ 📢 54   Listen to the description and label the diagram of a fire extinguisher.

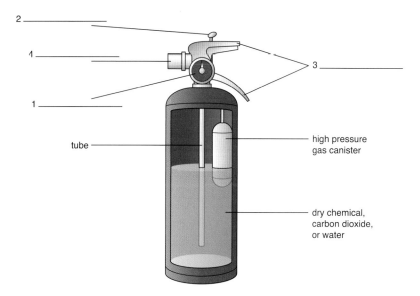

2 _____

4 _____

1 _____

3 _____

tube

high pressure gas canister

dry chemical, carbon dioxide, or water

**2**   Correct these sentences.

1   The fire extinguisher contains dry chemical, carbon dioxide <u>and</u> water.   *or*
2   The safety pin is under the pressure gauge.
3   The nozzle is on the right.
4   The tube is outside the container.
5   The gas canister is above the tube.

**3**   Complete this sentence.

When you squeeze the handle, …

**4**   Look at the chart. Underline the words for parts of a fire extinguisher. Match them to the labels in the diagram above.

| **(1)** HOLD UPRIGHT. PULL RING PIN. | **(2)** START BACK 10 FEET. AIM AT BASE OF FIRE. | **(3)** SQUEEZE LEVER, SWEEP SIDE TO SIDE. |

10 ft.

**5**   Practise in pairs. Take turns to explain how to use a fire extinguisher. Use the words in the box.

| pull | aim | squeeze | sweep |

# Incident reports

**Listening**    **1**    ▶ 🔊 55    Listen to four conversations. Complete the incident report forms.

Incident 1

Date: _10th January_       Time: _15:00_

Location: _Tank number_ _____

Description of incident: _Fire_ _____

Possible cause: _Faulty pressure_ _____

Action taken: _John Smith called the_ _____ _team_

Incident 2

Date: _14th March_       Time: _____

Location: _____

Description of incident: _____

Possible cause: _____

Action taken: _____

Incident 3

Date: _2nd August_       Time: _20:00_

Location: _____

Description of incident: _____

Possible cause: _____

Action taken: _____

Incident 4

Date: _31st October_       Time: _____

Location: _____

Description of incident: _____

Possible cause: _____

Action taken: _____

**Speaking**    **2**    Use the incident report forms to explain the incidents to a partner, but change some of the information. Your partner has to find the change. Then find a new partner and repeat.

# Talking about past incidents

1  Here are some questions from the conversations on page 56. Complete the words.

1  What happen_____ ?
2  What d_____ you do?
3  What caus_____ it?
4  How d_____ it happen?

## Language

### Past simple

| We use the **past simple** to talk about a completed action in the past. | *I called.* |
| --- | --- |
| | *He didn't call.* |
| | *Did you call?* |

| **Regular** | **Present** | **Past simple** | **Questions** | Did it work? |
| --- | --- | --- | --- | --- |
| | call | called | | Did he forget? |
| | roll | rolled | | Did he use water? |
| | ignite | ignited | | What happened? |
| | provide | provided | | What caused it? |
| | | | | How did it happen? |
| **Irregular** | **Present** | **Past simple** | | |
| | is / are (be) | was / were | | |
| | have | had | | |
| | forget | forgot | | |
| | come | came | | |
| | go | went | | |

2  Complete the sentences with the past simple tense of the verbs in brackets. Use the language box to help you.

1  The problem _____ (be) a faulty pressure gauge.
2  The detection system _____ (not work).
3  The alarm _____ (not go off).
4  I _____ (hear) you _____ (have) a problem.
5  Some fuel _____ (ignite).
6  He _____ (use) water instead of $CO_2$.
7  I _____ (turn on) the lights.
8  I _____ (call) the duty electrician.
9  The driver _____ (forget) to put the brakes on.
10  The tanker _____ (roll) into the wall.

**Speaking**  3  Now make up your own incident and describe it to a partner. They complete the incident form.

| | |
| --- | --- |
| Date: _____ | Time: _____ |
| Location: _____ | |
| Description of incident: _____ | |
| Possible cause: _____ | |
| Action taken: _____ | |

# In the storeroom

Listening **1** ▶ 🎧 56   Listen to five conversations in the storeroom. Complete the table.

| Conversation | What was asked for? |
|---|---|
| 1 | a tool box |
| 2 | |
| 3 | |
| 4 | |
| 5 | |

**2** ▶ 🎧 56   Complete the beginning of each conversation. Then listen again to check.

**Conversation 1**
A: How's it _____going_____ ?
B: OK, thanks.
A: I'm _____ for my tool box.

**Conversation 2**
B: Hello again. _____ OK?
A: Erm, this _____ my tool box.

**Conversation 3**
B: Hi.
C: Hi. I _____ a screwdriver.

**Conversation 4**
B: Hi, Joe.
D: Hi. How's it going?
B: Not _____ thanks. You?
D: Not bad. I'm off-shift in an hour. Do you have _____ ear protection?

**Conversation 5**
E: Morning. _____ day.
B: Yeah. What _____ I do for you?
E: I need _____ nuts.

Speaking **3** Turn to the audioscript for track 56 on page 76. Act out the conversations with different partners. Change how you speak to make the conversations more or less friendly.

**4** Practise in pairs. Have similar conversations. Take turns being the storekeeper.

# Review

**Writing** **1** Complete the crossword.

**Clues**

Across
1 Petroleum products that are light, strong and don't rust (8)
2 A plastic you cannot re-melt (9)
4 Fuel for aircraft (3, 4)
5 A place with lots of storage tanks (4, 4)
6 Another word for man-made (9)

Down
1 Another word for gasoline (6)
3 A vehicle used to transport fuel (4, 6)

**2** Complete the sentences with the verbs in the box.

| supply | provides | used | re-melted | is |
|---|---|---|---|---|

1 Synthetic rubber _is_____ a heat-resistant and corrosion-resistant material.
2 These tanks are _____ to store asphalt.
3 This facility _____ storage services for 35 different types of petrochemical.
4 We _____ automotive and industrial lubricants to customers all over the country.
5 Thermoplastics can be _____ .

**3** Write three sentences about plastics.

**4** Use the words in the box to describe an incident.

| door | smoke | fire alarm | extinguisher | telephone | supervisor |
|---|---|---|---|---|---|

**5** Complete the report form.

Date: _____    Time: _____

Location: _____

Description of incident: _____

_____

Possible cause: _____

_____

Action taken: _____

_____

# 8 Transport

- Talk about pipelines and pipeline jobs
- Describe types of oil tanker
- Use a vehicle maintenance checklist
- Talk about hobbies and interests

## Laying a pipeline

**Reading** **1** Look at the diagram and read the text.

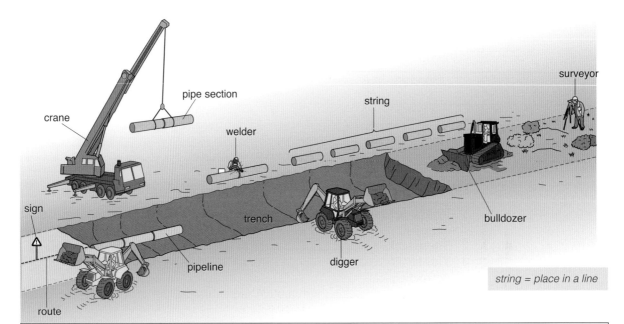

*string = place in a line*

Before work begins, two teams of surveyors travel along the route of the pipeline. One team drives along the route and the other team flies over the route by helicopter or small plane. They survey the whole route and inspect it carefully. After the survey, the work begins. First, workers drive bulldozers along the route and clear it. They take out trees, bushes and other obstacles and they level the ground. Next, they string pipes along the route. After this, the diggers dig trenches next to the pipe string. The trenches are about two metres deep. Then welders weld the pipes together into a pipe section. They also bend the pipe section into the shape of the route. Next, cranes lift up the pipe section and place it carefully into the trench. The welders then weld the section to the rest of the pipeline. Then diggers push earth into the trench and cover the pipeline. Workers place signs above the pipeline to warn the public. Finally, engineers pump water at high pressure through the complete pipeline. This tests the strength of the pipeline. If there is a leak, they will find it now.

**2** Make lists of the jobs and the vehicles in the text.

**Speaking** **3** Practise in pairs. Close your book. Describe the process of laying a pipe.

*First, surveyors travel along the route of the pipe. Then workers clear the route. After that …*

# Reporting progress

**Listening** 1   🔊 57   A company director (A) asks a project manager (B) to tell him about the company's pipeline project. Complete the conversation with the past simple tense of the verbs in brackets. Listen to check.

A: How's the pipeline? Can you bring me up to date, please?

B: Sure. We (1) _surveyed_____ (survey) the route last month. The bulldozers (2)_____ (finish) the path yesterday.

A: Good. Is the whole route (3)_____ (do) now?

B: Yes, it is.

A: That's good. What about the pipe sections?

B: We (4)_____ (start) last week. They (5)_____ (complete) the first 2 kilometres on Tuesday.

A: What about welding?

B: We (6)_____ (plan) to start welding last Friday but we (7)_____ (manage) to start on Thursday.

A: That's good. Well done.

**Speaking** 2   Underline the questions in this conversation. Read the conversation in pairs.

A: _How was the project?_ Did you finish on time?

B: Yes we did. Just!

A: How did you do it? I thought there were problems.

B: There were lots of problems but we had three extra crews.

A: I see. Where was it exactly? Somewhere in the US?

B: Yes, in Alaska. On the coast.

A: How did you get back? By boat?

B: No, by plane.

**Language**

### Past tense questions

| We use **questions** to get information. The word order in questions is different from positive and negative sentences and we can use special questions words. | **Did** you **finish** on time? |
| --- | --- |
| | **Did** you **have** any problems? |
| | **When did** the new valves arrive? |
| | **How did** you get back? |
| | **What was** the weather like? |

3   🔊 58   Complete this conversation. Listen to check.

A: We finished the repairs on the pipeline yesterday.

B: That's great. Ahead of schedule. When (1) _did_____ you finish the inspections?

A: On Tuesday.

B: I see. Did you (2)_____ any problems?

A: No, not really. A couple of small leaks. That's all. Nothing serious.

B: When (3)_____ the new valves arrive?

A: Before we left. So no problems there.

B: What (4)_____ the crew members like? Did you have a good supervisor?

A: Yes the team was very good and the supervisor was great.

**Speaking** 4   Practise in pairs. Student A turn to page 68. Student B turn to page 79.

# A pipeline route

**Reading**   **1**   Look at the photos and the map. Read the text.

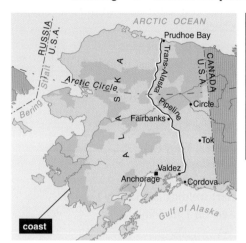

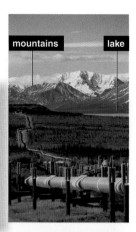

The Trans-Alaska Oil Pipeline is 800 miles long and goes from Prudhoe Bay to Valdez. It has 11 pump stations and took four years to build. Thousands of people worked on the project. It starts at the coast and finishes at the sea. It goes through valleys and crosses rivers.

**Listening**   **2**   🖸 **59**   Listen to an engineer talk about a planned pipeline route. How long is the route? What will happen on Monday?

       **3**   🖸 **59**   Listen again. Complete the sketch.

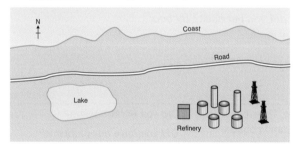

## Language

### will for talking about the future

| We use **will** + infinitive to talk about the future. | *The pipeline* **will go** *north-west around the lake.* |
| --- | --- |
| | *We'll (will)* **have** *a meeting to discuss the crews.* |
| | *It* **won't** *(will not)* **go** *south-west.* |
| | *What* **will happen** *on Monday?* |

**Speaking**   **4**   Practise in pairs. Student A draw a route for a pipeline from oil refinery A to the coast. Student B draw a route for a pipeline from oil refinery B to the coast. Don't show your partner. Take turns to describe your route for your partner to draw.

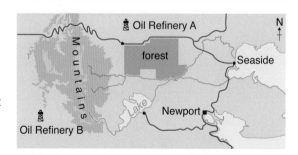

# Pipeline jobs

**Listening** **1** 🔊 **60** Listen to people talking about their jobs on the pipeline and complete the descriptions. Then match the descriptions to the pictures showing the jobs.

A

Crane operator

B [1]

Surveyor

C

Earthmoving machine operator

D

Engineer

E

Welder

F

Driver

1 My job is to help plan the _route_____ . I have a team of three to help me. We collect information about the land; we measure distances from point A to point B, for example, or we measure how high a point is above _____ level. We use this data to decide where to _____ the trenches and lay the pipe.

2 I drive and operate heavy equipment such as bulldozers and diggers. We _____ the route of obstacles like trees, _____ the ground and dig the trenches.

3 I look after the technical side. For example, I organise tests on the pipe to check that everything is OK and that there are no _____ .

4 My job is to join the _____ of pipe together. When I'm working, I use a special helmet to _____ my eyes.

5 I operate heavy machinery for moving equipment from A to B. For example, I lift sections of the pipe and _____ them in the trench.

6 My job is to transport the equipment and pipes from the ships to the site. Sometimes this means long _____ by road and across country. I also have to look after my _____ .

**2** 🔊 **61** Listen to three more job descriptions. Make notes.

1

Fitter

2

Pipeliner

3

Line walker

**Speaking** **3** Write down the name of a job in the oil industry. Do not show anybody. Then play 20 questions. Your teacher will explain how the game works.

# Oil tankers

**Language**

**Large numbers**
2,300 = two thousand, three hundred
300,000 = three hundred thousand
423,300 = four hundred and twenty-three thousand, three hundred

**1** 〔🎧 62〕 Listen to the information about oil tankers.
Match the numbers a–f to the correct words 1–6.

a) 4,000          1  metric tonnes
b) 320,000        2  width of *Jahre Viking*, in feet
c) 1,504          3  oil tankers
d) 226            4  length of *Jahre Viking*, in feet
e) 564,763        5  *Jahre Viking* scrapped
f) 2010           6  deadweight tonnage of
                     *Jahre Viking*

**2** 〔🎧 62〕 Listen again. Then answer these questions.

1  What is the difference between crude tankers and product tankers?
2  What does DWT stand for?
3  What does VLCC mean?

**Reading**  **3**  Here is some information about other classes of tanker. What do the words
*draft*, *beam* and *air draft* mean?

**Malaccamax**   The Strait of Malacca is 25 metres deep. Ships with a greater draft must find a
different route.
**Suezmax**   The Suez canal is 18–20 metres deep. There is another problem. The Suez Canal bridge is
68 metres high. The Suezmax class has a maximum DWT of 150,000.
**Panamax**   The width of the locks on the Panama canal limit the beam of the ship to 32 metres. The
maximum air draft, from waterline to the highest point of the ship, is 58 metres. The Panamax class is
typically between 65,000 and 80,000 DWT.
**Seawaymax**   The St Lawrence Seaway goes from the Great Lakes to the Atlantic Ocean. Seawaymax
ships can have a maximum length of 740 feet, a beam of 78 feet and a draft of 26 feet. Other ships on
the Great Lakes, called lake freighters, are larger than this and never leave the Great Lakes. They are
too large to pass through the locks of the St Lawrence Seaway.

**Speaking**  **4**  Work in pairs. Look at the tankers. Together decide which tankers can go
through the four locations described above.

A
Length: 340 m; Draft: 18 m; Beam: 44 m;
Air draft: 66 m; DWT: 200,000

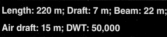

B
Length: 220 m; Draft: 7 m; Beam: 22 m;
Air draft: 15 m; DWT: 50,000

C
Length: 470 m; Draft: 23 m; Beam: 60 m;
Air draft: 72 m; DWT: 300,000

# Health and safety: Vehicle maintenance

**Listening** 1 🔊 63 Listen to the conversation. Complete the checklist.

**Vehicle maintenance checklist**

Name: _____

Date: _____

Location: _____

|  | Checked | Serviceable | Deficient | Action |
|---|---|---|---|---|
| Windscreen | ✓ | ✓ |  |  |
| Lights |  |  |  |  |
| Warning signs |  |  |  |  |
| Tyres |  |  |  |  |
| Discharge valves |  |  |  |  |
| Documents |  |  |  |  |

windscreen

warning sign

discharge valves

lights

tyres

**Writing** 2 You inspected a road tanker yesterday. Write three sentences about it. Use some of these words to write your report.

| check | inspect | warning signs | tyres | tread | discharge valves |
|---|---|---|---|---|---|
| lights | windscreen | documents | leaks | clean | missing | cracked |

*I checked the road tanker yesterday …*

**Speaking** 3 Work in pairs. Take turns to read your report to your partner. Add a sentence to your report. Then find another partner and repeat.

# Off-shift: Life on a supertanker

  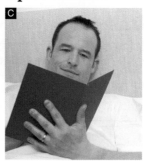 

**Listening**    **1**    🎧 **64**   William Tabone is a crew member on a supertanker. He works hard, especially when the ship is in port but he also has some free time. Listen to him talking about what he does when he is off-shift. Circle the activities you hear.

watch tv

play computer games

sleep

eat

listen to music

work out

read

write letters

play the guitar

go cycling

play games in the recreation room

go jogging

**2**    🎧 **64**   Listen again. What does William often do? What does he always do? And what does he do sometimes?

**3**    Make a list of your hobbies and interests. Use a dictionary or ask the teacher if you need help.

**Language**

| How often? | |
|---|---|
| We can use **adverbs of frequency** (e.g. *never, sometimes, often, normally, always*) and other **time expressions** (e.g. *once a week, every Sunday, twice a week, every day*) to say how often we do something. Adverbs of frequency come before the verb. Time expressions come at the beginning or end of the sentence. | *I **always** go to the cinema.* |
| | *He **sometimes** watches TV.* |
| | *I play football **every day**.* |
| | ***Every Sunday** I go to the cinema.* |

**Speaking**    **4**    Practise in pairs. Ask and answer questions about hobbies and interests. Tell the class what you find out.

*What do you do in your free time?*
*I like swimming. I normally go swimming every day.*
*He likes swimming. He normally goes swimming every day.*

# Review

Writing **1** Answer these questions.

1 What do diggers dig?
2 Who do supervisors supervise?
3 What do inspectors inspect?
4 What do drivers drive?
5 What do surveyors survey?
6 What do welders weld?

**2** What do these people do? Write a sentence for each job. Use the words in the box to help you.

| organise tests | operate heavy equipment | sections of pipe |
| measure distances | plan route | supervise | maintain pipe systems |

1 fitter          3 crane operator     5 welder
2 surveyor        4 engineer

**3** Write the words in the correct order to make questions.

1 check Did you the windscreen ?
2 you the Did inspect tyres ?
3 Did documents you look at the ?
4 did How you back get ?
5 go last Monday Did you ?
6 were What the members like crew ?

**4** Write down the route of the pipeline from the refinery to the coast.

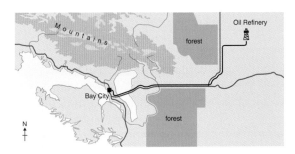

**5** Label this picture of a tanker with the words in the box. Then look back at page 64. What class of tanker is it?

| air draft | beam | draft |

Length: 280 m; Draft: 12 m; Beam: 31 m;
Air draft: 56 m; DWT: 75,000

**6** Write three to five sentences about your hobbies and interests.

*I like football. I usually play football on Friday.*

## 3 Oil fields

**Operating equipment** **Speaking exercise 4 page 21**

Tell your partner to write down these instructions.
1  Turn the handwheel anti-clockwise three turns.
2  Wait five minutes.
3  Check the gauge.
4  Write down the pressure on the gauge in the log book.
Then write down the instructions your partner gives you.

## 4 Drilling

**Health and safety:**
**Helicopters**
**Speaking exercise 4 page 33**

Ask your partner to explain how to board a helicopter.

**Off-shift in the canteen** **Speaking exercise 4 page 34**

You are the cashier in a canteen. Your partner is an oil worker. Use this information
and the menu on page 34 to answer his/her questions.

| Canteen opening times |
|---|
| 06:00–08:00, 12:00–14:00, 18:00–20:00, 24:00–02:00 |

## 5 Working offshore

**Dimensions** **Speaking exercise 3 page 38**

Convert the dimensions of pipe 2 into feet and inches
and write them in the table on page 38. Answer your
partner's questions about the dimensions of pipe 2 first
in metres and centimetres and then in feet and inches.
Then ask your partner questions about pipe 3. Complete
the table then check your partner's calculations.

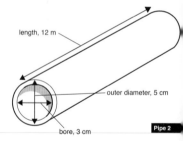

length, 12 m

outer diameter, 5 cm

bore, 3 cm

Pipe 2

## 6 Refining

**Health and safety:**
**Emergency procedures**
**Speaking exercise 5 page 49**

Phone your partner and report an emergency. Give your location and the type of
emergency. Choose one of these emergencies.

**Fire in the separation area**     **A leak in a piping system**

Then your partner will telephone you about an emergency. Write down his/her
name, job, location and the type of emergency. Ask questions if necessary.

## 8 Transport

**Reporting progress** **Speaking exercise 4 page 61**

You and your partner both finished a pipeline project
last week. Here are the details. Answer the questions
your partner asks you about your project. Use the details
in the box. Then ask your partner questions about their
project. Use the information in the box to help you.

| | |
|---|---|
| Location: | Mexico |
| Length: | 34 km |
| Start date: | 6th June |
| End date: | Last week |
| Weather: | Hot and rainy |
| Problems: | None |

## Unit 1 The oil industry

**02**

1 Hi. My name is Armando Panganiban. I'm from the Philippines. I'm a driver.
2 Hello. My name's Ricardo Cabrera. I'm from Venezuela. I'm a roustabout.
3 I'm Ali bin Khalid, from Saudi Arabia. I'm an engineer. Nice to meet you.
4 Hi, I'm Jennifer Burgess. I'm from Scotland. I'm a radio operator.
5 Hello. I'm Matthew Aondoakaa from Nigeria. I'm a seismic operator.

**03**

1 Hi. I'm Armando. I drive a road tanker from the refinery to the gas station. The gas station sells the gas.
2 Hi. This is Jennifer Burgess. We're on a supertanker. We transport oil.
3 Hello. My name's Matthew. My job is to search for oil. I work in the countryside.
4 I'm Ali bin Khalid. I work in a refinery.
5 Hi. This is Ricardo Cabrera. We work on an oil rig. We extract oil.

**04**

The alphabet
A, H, J, K
B, C, D, E, G, P, T, V, Z (American English)
F, L, M, N, S, X, Z (British English)
I, Y
O
Q, U, W
R

**05**

1 engineer: E-N-G-I-N-double E-R
2 operator: O-P-E-R-A-T-O-R
3 driver: D-R-I-V-E-R
4 roustabout: R-O-U-S-T-A-B-O-U-T
5 refinery: R-E-F-I-N-E-R-Y
6 oil rig: O-I-L, new word, R-I-G
7 tanker: T-A-N-K-E-R

**06**

1 A: Hello. My name's Cabrera. That's C-A-B-R-E-R-A.
   B: Thank you.

2 A: Panganiban.
   B: How do you spell that?
   A: It's Panganiban. P-A-N-G-A-N-I-B-A-N.
   B: Thank you.
3 A: Matthew Aondoakaa.
   B: Pardon?
   A: Aondoakaa. That's A-O-N-D-O-A-K-double A.
   B: Thank you.

**07**

PPE  RPM  VDU  USA  UAE

**08**

1 We transport the oil.
2 We extract the oil.
3 We search for oil.
4 We refine the oil.
5 I work on a super tanker.
6 We work on an oil rig.
7 We work in the countryside.
8 We work in the control room.
9 I'm the supervisor.
10 I'm the captain.
11 I'm a surveyor.
12 I'm a seismic operator.
13 I'm a driller.
14 I'm a control room operator.

**09**

**Conversation 1**
John: Hi. Welcome to the crew. My name's John. I'm the driller, so I'm in charge of this crew.
Ahmed: Thanks. I'm Ahmed.
John: This is Harry. And that's Martin. They're roughnecks.
Ahmed: Excuse me. Roughnecks?
John: Roughnecks. They do all the general jobs.
Ahmed: Oh, OK.

**Conversation 2**
Sayed: Hello. I'm Sayed. I'm the new control room operator.
Brian: Oh, good to see you, Sayed. I'm Brian. I'm the supervisor. This is Frank. He's an operator, too.
Sayed: Hi, Frank.
Frank: Hello, Sayed.

**Conversation 3**

Manuel: Hi. I'm looking for Fred. I'm Manuel.

Fred: Hi. I'm Fred. Are you the new radio operator?

Manuel: Yes, that's right.

Fred: Oh, good. Come with me. I'll show you the radio room.

**Conversation 4**

Antonio: Hello. My name's Antonio.

Chris: Pardon?

Antonio: Antonio.

Chris: Hi, Antonio. I'm Chris. Are you the new surveyor?

Antonio: Yes, that's right. Antonio Rivaldi.

Chris: Good to meet you. I'm a surveyor, too.

**10**

1 My gloves protect my hands.
2 These ear protectors are great.
3 My boots protect my feet.
4 My helmet protects my head.
5 Trousers protect my legs.
6 My safety glasses protect my eyes.
7 My jacket protects my body.

**11**

1 These are *my* ear protectors. Yours are over there.
2 My new boots are too big.
3 Where's my jacket?
4 Are these your safety glasses?
5 These trousers are too small. I need new ones.

**12**

1 Venezuela
2 Mexico
3 USA
4 Saudi Arabia
5 Kuwait
6 Alaska
7 Iraq
8 Russia

**13**

1 Samotlor is in Russia.
2 Prudhoe Bay? Alaska.
3 East Texas? That's in the USA.
4 Cantarell is in Mexico.
5 Greater Burgan is in Kuwait.
6 Rumaila is in Iraq.
7 The Ghawar oil field is in Saudi Arabia.
8 Bolivar Coastal is in Venezuela.

# Unit 2 Looking for oil

**14**

1 recording truck
2 shock waves
3 heavy plates
4 thumper truck
5 energy source
6 seismic operators

**15**

1 hydrophones
2 reflected
3 receiver
4 energy
5 explosives
6 different

**16**

A: Hi, Matthew.

B: Hi.

A: What do you do?

B: I'm a seismic operator.

A: What do seismic operators do?

B: Well, we search for oil.

A: OK.

B: And we work in crews, or teams. In my crew we have three surveyors and five seismic operators.

A: Right.

B: And two shooters.

A: Shooters?

B: That's right. Shooters.

A: What do they do?

B: They handle the explosives.

A: Oh, OK. I understand.

B: First, we survey the land. We look for the best places to go.

A: I see.

B: Then we clear the land. We remove trees and bushes, for example.

A: OK.

B: Then we do our tests. We operate thumper trucks. The heavy plates send shock waves into the rock. We use receivers to record the data and we use computers to analyse the data.

A: What about the shooters?

B: The shooters? Well, sometimes we don't use thumper trucks. Sometimes we use explosives. The shooters drill holes into the ground and prepare the site. Then they detonate the explosives. The explosives send shock waves through the rock. We use receivers to record the data from the shock waves. Then we use computers to analyse the data.

A: Do you like your job?

B: Yeah, I do.

## 17

a) 40
b) 13
c) 16
d) 22
e) 9

## 18

a) In our crew we have five people. The driller is in charge.
b) I work on a supertanker. We have a crew of 24.
c) We have four helmets. We need 13 pairs of gloves.
d) A: What is one plus four?
   B: Five.
e) A: What is three minus two?
   B: One.
f) A: How old are you?
   B: I'm 47. And you?
   A: I'm 36.
g) A: How tall are you?
   B: I'm six foot. And you?
   A: I'm five foot nine inches.
h) A: How heavy are you?
   B: I'm 79 kilos. And you?
   A: I'm 98 kilos.

## 19

Shooter: OK, your first job. Explosives are dangerous, so be careful.
Assistant: OK.
Shooter: First of all, turn off that phone. No phones with explosives.
Assistant: Sorry.
Shooter: No problem. Now. Bring the box over here.
Assistant: OK.
Shooter: And put the spare cables on the truck. Yellow on the right, red on the left.
Assistant: OK.
Shooter: And keep an eye on the road. Any cars, call me. OK?
Assistant: OK.
Shooter: And don't touch that flask. It's my coffee. Not yours!
Assistant: OK!

## 20

a) 0780 786 3487
b) 675 489 955
c) 546 389 2001

## 21

a) 030 3562 8788
b) 0071 253 528 998
c) 0049 756 463 339
d) 030 455 347 328
e) 0786 747 636 461

## 22

**Conversation 1**
A: What's your name?
B: Jason Henley.
A: Is Jason your given name?
B: Yes, Henley is my family name.
A: OK. Where do you live?
B: My address is 27 Port Drive, Aberdeen.
A: Did you say 27?
B: Yes, that's right.
A: And how old are you, please?
B: I'm 28.
A: 28? OK. Good. What's your job?
B: I'm a driller on an oil rig.
A: Thank you.

**Conversation 2**
A: What's your name, please?
B: John Karuett.
A: Can you spell that, please?
B: Yes, sure. It's John, J-O-H-N, Karuett, K-A-R-U-E-double T.
A: Thank you. And your address?
B: 45 Julienne Street.
A: OK. Postcode?
B: 24351.
A: Age?
B: 56.
A: Height?
B: Six foot one.
A: Weight?
B: 93 kilos.
A: OK. And what do you do?
B: I'm a shooter?
A: Pardon?
B: A shooter. I work with explosives.
A: OK. Thank you.

## Unit 3 Oil fields

**23**

1  well
2  pipe
3  tank
4  string
5  barrel
6  field
7  drill
8  hole
9  bit
10  collar

**24**

Supervisor:  OK. Listen carefully.
Trainee:  Understood.
Supervisor:  First, you turn this handwheel.
Trainee:  Clockwise?
Supervisor:  No, anti-clockwise.
Trainee:  OK, anti-clockwise.
Supervisor:  Turn it until it's open.
Trainee:  OK. Until it's open.
Supervisor:  Next, close this valve.
Trainee:  OK. Then close the valve.
Supervisor:  And then wait a couple of minutes.
Trainee:  Wait a couple of minutes.
Supervisor:  Then read the gauge and write the pressure in the log book.
Trainee:  OK. Got that.
Supervisor:  And finally, check the flanges and the valves.
Trainee:  For leaks?
Supervisor:  Yes, that's right.

**25**

a) three o'clock
b) three fifteen
c) four thirty
d) five forty
e) six forty-five
f) seven fifty

**26**

a) three forty
b) four forty
c) four forty-five
d) six fifteen
e) six fifty
f) seven thirty
g) seven thirty-five

**27**

1  A: What time are you off-shift?
   B: Six o'clock.
   A: Me too.

2  A: What time do we start?
   B: Two o'clock I think.
   A: OK.
3  A: What time do you finish?
   B: Seven o'clock.
   A: OK. See you in the canteen.
   B: Seven thirty, OK? I need a shower.
   A: Sure. Seven thirty is fine.
4  A: What time do you knock off?
   B: Eight fifteen.
   A: That's good. Meet you in the canteen.
   B: Oh sorry. Eight thirty today.
   A: OK.
5  A: What time do you start?
   B: Three o'clock. No, four o'clock.
   A: Good. Time for a cup of tea, then.

**28**

A: What time does the flight to Los Angeles leave?
B: At seven thirty-five.
A: What's the flight number?
B: TH3946.
A: What's the gate?
B: A1.
A: Is it on time?
B: Yes, it is.
A: Thank you.

**29**

1  A: What's this?
   B: It's a pressure gauge.
2  A: What's this for?
   B: It's for checking the temperature.
3  A: What does this switch do?
   B: It starts the engine.
4  A: How do I increase the speed?
   B: You turn the dial.
5  A: How do I lower the pressure?
   B: You open the valve.
6  A: What's this thing for?
   B: That's the power switch. It starts the motor.
7  A: Did you say turn the handle?
   B: Yes, that's right.
   A: Clockwise or anti-clockwise?
   B: Clockwise.
8  A: What do I do next?
   B: Press the start button.
   A: OK.

**30**

1  What's this for?
2  Did you say press the button?
3  What's this gauge for?
4  Did you say pull the lever?
5  What does this switch do?
6  Is this a start button?
7  Does this thing start the motor?

## 31

## Conversation 1
A: Where's Cantarell?
B: I think it's in Mexico.
A: Oh yes, thank you.
B: No problem.

## Conversation 2
A: Where's Greater Burgan?
B: I'm sure it's in Kuwait.
A: Oh, OK.

## Conversation 3
A: I think the pressure's too high.
B: Oh, yes, you're right. Open the valve.
A: OK. Good idea.

## Conversation 4
A: I think the temperature's too high.
B: I don't think you're right. 200 degrees is OK.
A: Are you sure?
B: OK, go and ask Jim.
A: OK. Will do.

## Conversation 5
A: Where's your hard hat?
B: In my room. Why?
A: Go and get it. You must wear a hard hat in this area.
B: Oh, OK. I didn't know that. Sorry.

## Conversation 6
A: Cup of tea?
B: Good idea.
A: Milk and sugar?
B: Yes, please.

## Conversation 7
A: Don't touch the flask.
B: Why? Is it yours?
A: No, it's Norman's.
B: Oh, fair enough.

# Unit 4 Drilling

32

1 First, attach the drill pipe to the drill bit.
2 Second, put the collar on the drill bit.
3 Third, fix the kelly to the drill pipe.
4 After that, trip the drill string into the well hole.
5 Next, slide the kelly into the turntable.
6 Then, turn on the power.
7 Next, drill the hole.
8 After that, attach another drill pipe to the string. Then, drill again.
9 Then, trip the drill string out of the well hole.
10 Finally, install the casing in the well hole.

33

1 The swivel hangs from a hook.
2 The kelly connects the swivel to the drill pipe.
3 The kelly goes through the turntable.
4 The engines turn the turntable.
5 The turntable rotates.
6 The turntable turns the kelly.
7 The kelly turns the drill pipe.

34

## Conversation 1
A: OK. Let's see. First thing is to undo the flange. Pass me the pipe wrench, please.
B: What size?
A: 40 cm should do it.
B: OK.

## Conversation 2
A: It's not moving.
B: No problem. Give me the sledgehammer.
A: OK.

## Conversation 3
A: Right. Now I need the pliers.
B: Which ones?
A: The needle-nose, please. They're next to the flask.
B: Ah, got them. Here you are.
A: Thanks.

35

Where's the supervisor's office?
1 It's at the end of the corridor.
2 It's down the corridor, on the right.
3 It's along the corridor, third door on the left.
4 It's through the door.
Where's the car park?
5 Go through the gate. The car park is on the left.
6 Drive past the trees. It's on the right.
7 It's next to the derrick.
8 It's opposite the pumpjack.
9 It's between the derrick and the pumpjack.

36

Here are some instructions. First of all, remove any loose items which might blow away. Always approach a helicopter where the pilot can see you. The tail rotor is dangerous. Get in the helicopter only when the pilot signals you to do so. Fasten your seatbelt as soon as you are seated and put on your ear protection. This flight is over water so you must wear a survival suit and a lifejacket.

37

## Conversation 1
A: Hi. I'd like some fries, please, and a cola.
B: Here you are. That's one dollar.
A: Thank you.

**Conversation 2**

A: Hello.

B: Hello. What would you like?

A: Could I have a pizza and a glass of water, please?

B: Here you are. That's seven thirty-five, please.

A: Here's ten.

B: That's two fifty-five change.

A: Thank you.

**Conversation 3**

A: Hi. I'd like some soup and a beefburger, please. Oh, and a glass of orange juice.

B: Sure. Here you are. Five fifty, please.

A: Thank you. Here's six. Keep the change.

B: Thanks.

A: You're welcome. Have a nice day now.

# Unit 5 Working offshore

**38**

A: What's this?

B: It's a derrick.

A: What does it do?

B: It supports the block.

A: Did you say the block?

B: Yes, that's correct.

**39**

A: Does the motor turn the turntable?

B: Yes, it does.

A: And the engines? Do the engines provide the power?

B: Yes, they do.

A: Does the pump drive the generator?

B: No, it doesn't. The engines drive the generator.

A: Do the tanks on the left hold water?

B: No, they don't. They hold fuel.

**40**

1   The engines provide the power.
2   The fuel tanks hold fuel for the engines.
3   The engines drive the generator.
4   The generator provides electrical power for the motor and the pump.
5   The pump sucks mud from the mud pit.
6   The motor turns the turntable.
7   The water tank holds water for the mud pit.
8   The mud pit contains the drilling fluid.
9   The pipe racks support the drill pipes.

**41**

A: How long is this pipe?

B: It's 30 feet long.

A: Did you say 30 feet?

B: Yes, that's correct.

A: What's that in metres?

B: About 10 metres.

A: OK. What's the diameter?

B: The outside diameter is 6 inches. The wall thickness is half an inch. And, before you ask, an inch is about two and a half centimetres. So that's about 15 centimetres outside diameter and a wall thickness of just over a centimetre.

A: So the bore is about 12.5 centimetres.

B: That's right.

A: OK, thank you.

B: You're welcome.

**42**

1   One foot is equal to 12 inches.
2   One inch is about two point five centimetres.
3   One metre is about three feet.

**43**

A: Tell me about the platform. How much oil does it produce?

B: It produces about 21,000 barrels per day.

A: How many tonnes is that per year?

B: Let me see. That's over one million tonnes per year.

A: How many oil workers are there on the platform?

B: I think there are about 120.

A: How much money do the oil workers earn?

B: They earn quite a lot because they have to work away from home.

**44**

**Conversation 1**

A: What's the problem?

B: I have this cough.

A: OK, here's some cough medicine. NEXT!

**Conversation 2**

A: What's the matter?

B: Too much sun. Sunburn.

A: OK, you need sun cream. Here you are. NEXT!

**Conversation 3**

A: What's up?

B: My head hurts. I have a headache.

A: Headache? OK. Take these pills. One every four hours. NEXT!

**Conversation 4**

A: What's the problem?

B: My back. I hurt my back.

A: Hmm. OK. Wait in the other room. NEXT!

**Conversation 5**

A: What's up?

B: I've got something in my eye.

A: Let's see. OK. Here are some eye drops. NEXT!

**Conversation 6**

A: Hi. What's the matter?

B: I hurt my hand.

A: Hmm, OK. I'll do an X-ray.

1 OK, the recreation room. There's a TV, a snooker table, a telephone and some books. There's also a notice board.
2 The mess area? Just tables and chairs and a window to the galley.
3 The galley? It's a kitchen. It's where we cook our food.
4 The fitness room? We have a running machine and some other sports equipment.
5 The washing machines are on all the time. We get very dirty in this job.
6 Everyone has a locker. That's where we keep our PPE.

# Unit 6 Refining

1 It's two thirty.
A: Good morning.
B: Good afternoon.
A: Erm, afternoon I mean. I'm here to see Dr Schmidt.
B: Name, please?
A: Hans Clements.
B: Could I see your ID card, please?
A: Of course. Here you are.
B: Thank you. That's fine, Mr Clements. Now, let me see. Dr Schmidt. Oh, OK. Building 51. It's near the river.
A: Thank you.
2 It's two thirty-five.
A: Hi.
B: Hi. How can I help you?
A: My name's Abdullah Al-Rakhis. I'm from the fire department. I'm here to check the hazmat area.
B: OK. Do you know where it is?
A: Yes, thanks.
3 It's two forty-five.
A: Hello.
B: Good afternoon.
A: Erm, good afternoon. I'm Sally Digby. I'm new. I need to go to Building 43.
B: Do you have any identification, please?
A: Yes, of course. Here's my passport.
B: Oh, OK. The admin buildings are over there, on the left, Ms Digby.
A: Thank you.
4 It's three o'clock.
A: Hi. Marisa Codreanu and Dennis Poljakovic. We're here to inspect one of the distillation towers.
B: Dr Rogers runs the separation area. One moment, please. I'll call her.

A: Thank you.
5 It's three fifteen.
A: Hello. I have some spare parts for the control room.
B: What's your name, please?
A: Liu Gaoxuan. From GZ Electronics.
B: Liu Gaoxuan? Can you spell that, please?
A: Liu. L-I-U. Gaoxuan. G-A-O-X-U-A-N.
B: Thank you. One moment, please.
6 It's three twenty.
A: Hi. I'm Connie Grieve from the Water and Electricity department. You have a problem with your substation.
B: One moment, please.
A: OK.

OK, so this refinery is nearly three kilometres long and about one kilometre wide, so it covers an area of about three square kilometres. We're now in the control room. This is the centre of the refinery. Everything is controlled from here. We have three gates, with a parking area near each gate. We control access at the gates. Electricity is provided by the substation. Water comes from the river. We use a lot of water to make our products.
The refinery is divided into three main areas. The separation area, with the distillation columns, is where we separate the crude oil into different components. The conversion area is where we use heat and pressure to change the components. The treatment area is where we add chemicals to make the final products. The buildings in the treatment area are the labs.

**Conversation 1**
A: What's today?
B: Tuesday.
A: Ah, Thanks.
**Conversation 2**
A: Is today Thursday?
B: No, it's Friday.
A: Oh, great.

January, February, March, April, May, June, July, August, September, October, November, December

Right. In an emergency the first thing you do is raise the alarm. Shout 'Fire! Fire! Fire!'. Second, if possible, call the emergency services. Third, switch off all the machines and go to an assembly area. Then, check all your people are present Finally, report to the senior person. OK. Any questions?

1  It's raining.
2  It's windy.
3  It's a storm. Listen to the thunder.

1  It's very cold today. It's twenty below and it's snowing.
2  It's freezing. It's zero degrees. There's ice on the roads.
3  It's a nice day. It's 20 degrees. No rain today.
4  It's very hot today. It's 40 degrees. It's very windy.

# Unit 7 Storage

1  These tanks are used to store asphalt. The tanks are heated to keep the asphalt at the right temperature.
2  This depot is for storage only. We don't do any processing here. On the left you can see the tanks and the gantries which allow us to pump the products into road tankers. Tanks 1, 2 and 3 are the largest and are for diesel fuels. Tank 4, the smallest, is for kerosene, and tanks 5 and 6 are for fuel oils.
3  We are one of the largest storage facilities in this part of China. This facility provides storage services for 35 different types of petrochemical. Most of the petrochemicals are used as feedstock for other processes.
4  This tank farm was built 20 years ago, so it's one of our oldest facilities. We have 134 tanks now. We supply automotive and industrial lubricants to customers all over the country. We can handle up to 60 tankers an hour.
5  The bullet tanks you can see all store liquefied petroleum gas, or LPG, in this case propane or butane. We have additional capacity in underground tanks which are behind the control room.

This is a typical fire extinguisher. The pressure gauge shows the pressure. At the top is a safety pin. To use the extinguisher first pull the safety pin. When you squeeze the handle, dry chemical, carbon dioxide or water goes up the tube and comes out of the nozzle.

## Incident 1

A: I heard you had an incident. One of the tanks, right?
B: Tank number 3. I think the problem was a faulty pressure gauge. The detection system didn't work and the alarm didn't go off.
A: Oh.
B: We were lucky. John Smith saw the smoke and called the fire team out. And they were fast.
A: Ah, That's good!

## Incident 2

A: I heard you had a problem.
B: Yeah. Last night, around three o'clock. In Building 4. Well, two problems really.
A: What happened?
B: Some fuel ignited. Must have been a faulty switch or something. Anyway, the labourer used the wrong extinguisher on the fire. He used water instead of $CO_2$.
A: But that's crazy. Everyone knows not to put water on burning fuel.
B: Yeah, I know. Anyway, we extinguished the fire.

## Incident 3

A: So what caused the incident exactly?
B: There was an electrical problem, I think. In one of the asphalt tanks. I turned on the lights and there was a flash and some smoke.
A: So what did you do?
B: I called the duty electrician. He came straightaway.

## Incident 4

A: I saw the broken wall near the main gate. How did it happen?
B: Not sure. We think the driver forgot to put the brakes on. Maybe he was tired. I don't know. But the tanker rolled into the wall.
A: Anyone hurt?
B: No, luckily. Just a broken wall.
A: What time was all this?
B: About six a.m.
A: This morning?
B: No, yesterday. We called Maintenance.

## Conversation 1

A: How's it going?
B: OK, thanks.
A: I'm here for my tool box. I left it here last week.
B: What's your name?
A: Smith.
B: Oh, yes. Smith. Here you are.
A: Thank you.
B: You're welcome.

**Conversation 2**

B: Hello again. Everything OK?

A: Erm, this isn't my tool box.

B: Sorry?

A: These aren't my tools. My tools are new. These are old.

B: Are you Jeff Smith? Jeff with a 'J'?

A: No Geoff with a 'G'.

B: Oh, I see. My mistake. One moment, please.

A: Thanks.

B: Here you are.

A: Thanks.

**Conversation 3**

B: Hi.

C: Hi. I need a screwdriver.

B: No problem. What type?

C: Three-quarter inch, flat blade.

B: Just a sec. Here you are.

C: Thanks.

**Conversation 4**

B: Hi, Joe.

D: Hi. How's it going?

B: Not bad, thanks. You?

D: Not bad. I'm off-shift in an hour. Do you have any ear protection?

B: Yes sure. What sort? We have ear plugs, ear defenders, ear defenders for a helmet and ear defenders with a radio fitted.

D: Er. Just ear defenders, please.

B: OK. Here you are.

**Conversation 5**

E: Morning. Nice day.

B: Yeah. What can I do for you?

E: I need some nuts.

B: Nuts we got. What type?

E: Three-quarter inch. Coarse thread, please. And half inch. Coarse, too.

B: How many?

E: Two of each, please.

B: OK, just a sec. OK, half inch, no problem. Looks like we're right out of three-quarter inch. Sorry.

E: Can you order some?

B: No problem. They'll be here tomorrow.

E: Thanks.

# Unit 8 Transport

**57**

A: How's the pipeline? Can you bring me up to date, please?

B: Sure. We surveyed the route last month. The bulldozers finished the path yesterday.

A: Good. Is the whole route done now?

B: Yes, it is.

A: That's good. What about the pipe sections?

B: We started last week. They completed the first 2 kilometres on Tuesday.

A: What about welding?

B: We planned to start welding last Friday but we managed to start on Thursday.

A: That's good. Well done.

**58**

A: We finished the repairs on the pipeline yesterday.

B: That's great. Ahead of schedule. When did you finish the inspections?

A: On Tuesday.

B: I see. Did you have any problems?

A: No, not really. A couple of small leaks. That's all. Nothing serious.

B: When did the new valves arrive?

A: Before we left. So no problems there.

B: What were the crew members like? Did you have a good supervisor?

A: Yes, the team was very good and the supervisor was great.

**59**

A: OK. The route is simple. The pipeline will go from the refinery to the coast. It's a distance of about 25 kilometres. OK?

B: From the refinery to the coast?

A: Yeah. The first section will go straight west from the refinery to the lake.

B: Straight west, OK.

A: Section two will go north-west around the lake and cross the road here.

B: North-west to the road?

A: Yeah. It crosses the road and section three will then follow a straight line north to the coast.

B: Straight north, OK.

A: Any questions?

B: No, that's fine.

A: OK, good. We'll have a meeting next week to discuss the schedule and the crews. OK?

B: When next week?

A: On Monday. In my office at ten.

B: I'll be there.

A: Great. OK. Thank you.

B: You're welcome. See you next week.

**60**

1 My job is to help plan the route. I have a team of three to help me. We collect information about the land; we measure distances from point A to point B, for example, or we measure how high a point is above sea level. We use this data to decide where to dig the trenches and lay the pipe.

2  I drive and operate heavy equipment such as bulldozers and diggers. We clear the route of obstacles like trees, level the ground and dig the trenches.

3  I look after the technical side. For example, I organise tests on the pipe to check that everything is OK and that there are no leaks.

4  My job is to join the sections of pipe together. When I'm working, I use a special helmet to protect my eyes.

5  I operate heavy machinery for moving equipment from A to B. For example, I lift sections of the pipe and put them in the trench.

6  My job is to transport the equipment and pipes from the ships to the site. Sometimes this means long distances by road and across country. I also have to look after my truck.

▶ 🎧 61

1  I'm a fitter. My main job is to prepare the pipe sections for welding. I also install and maintain pipe systems such as gauges and other measuring instruments.

2  My job's a pipeliner. I do lots of different tasks. Sometimes I help the surveyors or the heavy machine operators or the fitters. Sometimes I have to help clear the route of obstacles or fill in the trenches. And sometimes I clean storage tanks. It's heavy work, normally.

3  I'm a line walker. My job starts when the pipeline is finished. I use a car or I go on foot and I check the pipeline for leaks or other problems. Sometimes I can fix the problem myself and sometimes I report the problem to the engineers.

▶ 🎧 62

Crude tankers carry crude oil from drill sites to refineries. Product tankers carry petroleum products from the refineries to the market. There are over 4,000 oil tankers of 1,000 DWT or greater worldwide. DWT stands for dead-weight tonnage. Tankers come in different sizes and classes. The largest are called ultra large crude carriers, or ULCCs for short. They can carry DWTs of 320,000 metric tonnes or more. Very large crude carriers, or VLCCs, carry between 200,000 and 320,000 DWT. The longest tanker in the world, *Jahre Viking*, also known as *Seawise Giant*, *Happy Giant* and *Knock Nevis*, was 1,504 feet long and 226 feet wide and could carry 564,763 DWT. She was scrapped in 2010.

🎧 63

A: OK, so let's see. Did you check the windscreen? Check it's clean and look for any damage.
B: Yes, looks OK.
A: OK, good. What about the lights? All clean and working?
B: Yes, OK.
A: Good. Warning signs?
B: Side warning signs OK. Rear warning sign missing.
A: Missing?
B: Yes. Looks like someone took it.
A: OK. We need to get a new one then.
B: Yes.
A: OK. Tyres? Check for damage. Check the tread and the pressure.
B: All OK.
A: Discharge valves? Any leaks?
B: No leaks. But number 3 is cracked. The others are all OK.
A: Hmm. OK. Documents?
B: All OK.
A: Good, so let's get go and get a cup of coffee.

🎧 64

A: What do you do when you're off-shift?
B: In my free time I do lots of things. I often watch TV, I always sleep, I sometimes read, I listen to music. I also like playing the guitar.
A: What sort of music do you like?
B: I like most sorts of music.
A: What about exercise?
B: The ship has a fitness room, so I work out most days.
A: I see.
B: I also like cycling and jogging.
A: Cycling? In the fitness room?
B: No, on a real bicycle. The ship is over 300 metres long, so I can go cycling and jogging every day, except when the weather is bad, of course.

## 3 Oil fields

**Operating equipment** **Speaking exercise 4 page 21**

Write down the instructions your partner gives you.

Then tell your partner to write down these instructions.

1  Check the valve for leaks.
2  Open the valve.
3  Turn the handwheel clockwise three turns.
4  Telephone the supervisor and tell him the pressure.

## 4 Drilling

**Health and safety:
Helicopters**

**Speaking exercise 4 page 33**

Ask your partner to draw a helicopter and name the parts.

**Off-shift in the
canteen**

**Speaking exercise 4 page 34**

You are an oil worker in a canteen. Your partner is the cashier. Ask what time the canteen opens and closes. Use the menu on page 34 to order a meal. Ask how much it costs.

## 5 Working offshore

**Dimensions**

**Speaking exercise 3 page 38**

Convert the dimensions of pipe 3 into feet and inches and write them in the table on page 38. Ask your partner questions about pipe 2. Complete the table then check your partner's calculations. Then answer your partner's questions about the dimensions of pipe 3 first in metres and centimetres and then in feet and inches.

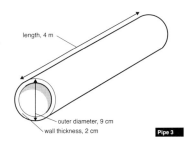

length, 4 m

outer diameter, 9 cm

wall thickness, 2 cm

Pipe 3

## 6 Refining

**Health and safety:
Emergency procedures**

**Speaking exercise 5 page 49**

Your partner will telephone you about an emergency. Write down his/her name, job, location and the type of emergency. Ask questions if necessary. Then phone your partner and report an emergency. Give your location and the type of emergency. Choose one of these emergencies.

**Smoke in a lab**          **A problem at the substation**

## 8 Transport

**Reporting progress**

**Speaking exercise 4 page 61**

You and your partner both finished a pipeline project last week. Here are the details. Ask your partner questions about their project. Use the information in the box to help you. Then answer the questions your partner asks you. Use the details in the box.

| | |
|---|---|
| Location: | Alaska |
| Length: | 102 km |
| Start date: | 30th September |
| End date: | Last week |
| Weather: | Cold and wet |
| Problems: | Only the weather |

**Pearson Education Limited**
Edinburgh Gate
Harlow
Essex CM20 2JE
England

and Associated Companies throughout the world.

www.pearsonlongman.com

First published 2011

ISBN: 978-1-4082-6997-8

Set in ITC Cheltenham Book

Printed and bound by Graficas Estella, Spain

Design: Pearson Education

**Acknowledgements**

The publishers and authors would like to thank the following people and institutions for their feedback and comments during the development of the material:

Pamela Heath, Canada; Daniel Mangrum, UAE; Schona Playford, Qatar; Paul Rogers, Saudi Arabia

The publisher would like to thank the following for their kind permission to reproduce their photographs:

(Key: b-bottom; c-centre; l-left; r-right; t-top)

**p4: Alamy Images:** Danny Hooks (B); artpartner-images.com (D). **Fotolia.com:** time2lime (A). **Photolibrary.com:** Red Chopsticks (E). **STILL Pictures The Whole Earth Photo Library:** Julio Etchart (C). **p7: Alamy Images:** Archie Miles (B). **Art Directors and TRIP Photo Library:** Dimitri Mossienko (A). **Photolibrary.com:** Larry Lee Photography (C). **Pictures courtesy of BP plc:** (D). **p9: Alamy Images:** Artostock.com (trousers); numb (jacket). **DK Images:** Stephen Oliver (helmet). **iStockphoto:** (glasses). **Thinkstock. p12: Alamy Images:** artpartner-images.com. **p14: Photolibrary. com:** Corbis. **p16: iStockphoto:** (bottle). **Thinkstock:** iStockphoto (mobile phone, pen); Jeffrey Hamilton (keys); Hemera (cupboard); Jupiterimages / Creatas (window). **p21: Alamy Images:** Stock Connection Distribution. **p23: Alamy Images:** Nuno André. **p24: Alamy Images:** artpartner-images.com (br). **Getty Images:** Steven Puetzer (bc). **iStockphoto:** (gloves). **Photolibrary.com:** Javier Larrea / age fotostock (t/gauge). **Science Photo Library Ltd:** Chris Sattlberger (bl). **Thinkstock:** iStockphoto (helmet); Hemera (valve). **p30: iStockphoto:** (br). **STILL Pictures The Whole Earth Photo Library:** Design Pics (bl). **Thinkstock:** (bc). **p31: Alamy Images:** Eye-Stock (screwdriver); SCPhotos (paint); RJH_RF (hole). **iStockphoto** (nail, screw, wire). **Pearson Education Ltd:** Gareth Boden (hammer). **Thinkstock:** Brand X Pictures (paint brush, wrench); Comstock (drill); Hemera (nut). **p33: STILL Pictures The Whole Earth Photo Library:** Graham Eaton. **p37: Getty Images:** Harald Sund. **p38: Photolibrary.com:** A Farnsworth / age fotostock. **p41: Pictures courtesy of BP plc. p44: Alamy Images:** picturesbyrob (l); Gabe Palmer (c); Dimitri Mossienko / Art Directors & TRIP (r). **p45: Photolibrary.com:** Corbis. **p46: Photolibrary.com. p47: Thinkstock:** iStockphoto. **p49: Corbis:** STRINGER / IRAQ / Reuters. **p50: Rex Features:** KPA / Zuma. **p52: Alamy Images:** Alvis Upitis (C). **Art Directors and TRIP Photo Library:** Helene Rogers (D). **Getty Images:** Robyn Beck / AFP (A). **Photolibrary.com:** Red Chopsticks (B); (E). **p53: Alamy Images:** AfriPics.com (C). **iStockphoto:** (A, B). **Photolibrary.com:** Nick Daly (D). **Thinkstock:** Hemera (E). **p56: Getty Images:** Code Red. **p58: Alamy Images:** Oliver Leedham. **p59: Alamy Images:** FirePhoto. **p62: Photolibrary.com:** Ken Graham / age fotostock (t); Steve Kaufman / Peter Arnold Images (b). **p63: Alamy Images:** Kevpix (1, C); Accent Alaska. com (2); Harry Stewart (D). **Getty Images:** Oleg Nikishin (A). **Photolibrary.com:** Peter & Georgina Bowater (E); Alan Kearney / age fotostock (3). **Rex Features:** Gary Leighty (B); OJO Images (F). **p64: www.fotoflite.com. p65: Alamy Images:** Mar Photographics. **p66: Alamy Images:** Beyond Fotomedia GmbH (C). **Art Directors and TRIP Photo Library:** Spencer Grant (A). **Getty Images:** Vincent J. Ricardel (B). **Rex Features:** Burger / Phanie (D). **p67: www.fotoflite.com**

**Cover images:** *Front:* **Fotolia.com:** Carabay (c); **iStockphoto:** Christian Lagereek Background, George Clerk (r), Ricardo Azoury (l)

All other images © Pearson Education